C000070823

Moseley into the Millennium

The Story of Moseley School

Project No: S11552
Moseley School
Birmingham City
Architects

January 1995

Moseley School
Wake Green Road
Moseley
Birmingham

Sectional perspective of
library showing proposed
structural works to wall
and roof

Moseley into the Millennium

The Story of Moseley School

Celia Gaskin
Meriel Vlaeminke
Katharine Gaskin

BREWIN
BOOKS

First published in 1998 by
Brewin Books, Studley, Warwickshire B80 7LG

© Celia Gaskin, Meriel Vlaeminke
and Katharine Gaskin 1998

All rights reserved.

British Library Cataloguing in Publication Data
A catalogue record for this book is available from
The British Library

ISBN: 1 85858 121 4

Typeset in New Century Schoolbook and made and printed
in Great Britain by Warwick Printing Company Limited,
Theatre Street, Warwick, Warwickshire CV34 4DR.

This book is dedicated to the memory of Bruce Gaskin, a wonderful father and a wonderful headmaster.

Line drawings from original photographs by Celia Gaskin.
Cover design by Keith James.

Authors' Note

Whilst every effort has been made to track down and check information, we are aware that there is more to find. Moseley School is establishing a permanent archive and would welcome any further contributions to its story. The authors would like to make it clear that any opinions expressed, other than those quoted from other sources, are their own and not those of the school.

Many people have helped us with this book; we have tried to acknowledge all their contributions. We would, however, particularly like to thank the following:

      Roy Holloway ~ Archivist to the Moseleians Association

      Peter Bassett ~ Project Architect for Birmingham Design Services

      Peter Anstey ~ Deputy Head of Moseley School
and finally:

      Betty Gaskin ~ who has lived through every moment of it with us!

Celia Gaskin BA
Meriel Vlaeminke (nee Gaskin) PhD
Katharine Gaskin PhD
July 1998

FOREWORD

It really was the big school and it hit you as such as you approached the entrance in Wake Green Road. It didn't matter that you'd passed Moseley Grammar School dozens of time before because never before had it had this impact upon you. Induction days had not been thought of, and so there was no opportunity for you to visit the school in the term before you started so that you could get a feel for it. Instead, and as everyone rightly warned, you were plunged from a small pond into a big pool. As you waved weakly to your dad who'd decided he'd back you up on this nervy day by walking up to Windermere Road with you, the collywobbles started to gush around your stomach just as your arms and legs stiffened into pin-like objects.

Looking around for someone from your old school, you were crestfallen to find only a press of unfamiliar faces. Then it was through the entrance and as you came towards the 1st and 2nd form playground – or quad as you were soon instructed it was to be called – a big lad sprang from the wall and snatched the cap from your head. Instinctively you tried to grab it back as he circled you triumphantly. You couldn't get near him and the more you strove the more you had to battle to make sure that nothing glistened in your eyes. What a relief when an even bigger kid, a lad who'd been above you in your old school, came to your rescue and tugged back your cap just as the bell rang for you to make your way to your form room – 1Z, the last classroom in the building which swung outwards towards Pickwick Grove.

With registration finished you safely pushed something called a record book into the satchel your Nan had bought you to show you how proud she was that you were the first one in your family ever to go to a grammar school. And you wished that she, or your mom or dad, or someone could have let you know what to expect. Because at the end of each lesson a bell rang and you had to find the class of the next teacher, bobbing and weaving as you went down the main corridor hoping that you'd find the right way. Now it was Latin and as you sat fretting about a language about which you knew nothing a man walked into the classroom. As he did so he said 'ambulo'. When he reached a chair he sat down and said 'sedeo'. Then he stood up and left the classroom. You looked around hopelessly, catching the eyes of other bewildered youngsters, and then the man came back again and went through the same process. Suddenly you realised that ambulo had something to do with walking and sedeo was connected to sitting.

Later you found out that the man's name was Dave Martin and he proved to be one of the finest teachers you ever met, a man with a talent for bringing to life a dead language. He wasn't on his own in his abilities. There was Bertie Briscoe, who drew you into the sounds and ways of Spanish; Mr Dolman and Mr Flood, who encouraged you to debate religion with them; Mrs Bradshaw, who cajoled and convinced you to read books in English that you would never have taken up; Harry Hopwood and Mr Stewart who shared your love of history and who cheered it on; and Pancho Pearson, a wonderful French teacher who gave so much of himself and his time to those whom he taught both in the classroom and outside it.

As time went on you came to appreciate the school and its ways, although you never understood why you couldn't have a football team and why you had to play rugby. And when Moseley Grammar School ceased to be and merged with the former Moseley Modern School, you realised that both schools were filled with devoted teachers and talented students. Now Moseley School, the same features are as obvious today. Moseley School carries on doing successfully what its predecessors did effectively: providing a place for youngsters to develop their abilities and fulfil their dreams. As the millennium approaches, it is certain it will carry on doing the job it does so well.

Carl Chinn

Department of Modern History
University of Birmingham

CONTENTS

Introduction

This book tells the story of Moseley School, its buildings and the people who have lived and worked in them from the mid-nineteenth century until the present day. It is an intriguing history of innovation, survival and growth, set within the social and educational context of the last 150 years. The story began in 1857 when a group of leading Nonconformists acquired a site in rural Wake Green Road for the expansion of their training college for ministers. The book describes the mixed fortunes of this establishment and traces the origins of today's Moseley School from the turn of the century College Road Board School.

Using a wide range of historical sources, the book charts the evolution of College Road School, Moseley Secondary (Grammar) School, Moseley Modern School and the comprehensive school of today. It also records the dramatic story of the magnificent gothic-style Victorian building which, through neglect, came to the brink of demolition but in 1998 is now restored to its original splendour. The book is published to coincide with the celebration of the re-opening of this part of Moseley School as Spring Hill College for post-16 and community use. But the original Spring Hill College began in very different surroundings.

Birmingham had grown by the middle of the nineteenth century from a successful market town into a major industrial centre, notable for the number of manufacturers who by inventive practices and sheer hard work, made fortunes out of the expert production of everyday items like screws, wire, pens, glass and buttons, as well as the specialist trades of jewellery and gun making. With the industrial expansion of Birmingham came the problems associated with rapid population growth: overcrowding and poor housing, inadequate provision for public health, a death rate of more than 25 per cent per annum, and minimal provision of basic services such as a water supply, sewerage system, paving, street cleaning and policing.

Politically, perhaps more than any city, Birmingham exemplified the need for reform. It lacked representation in Parliament until 1832 when it became a parliamentary borough, and there was no effective form of local government until after 1851 when the municipal borough created in 1838 began to function properly. Only then could the city's leaders begin to tackle its daunting problems.

As Birmingham city centre became less and less congenial, those who could afford it were moving out to healthier districts, particularly on the south and west sides. The parish of Yardley, on the southern side, was still in the County

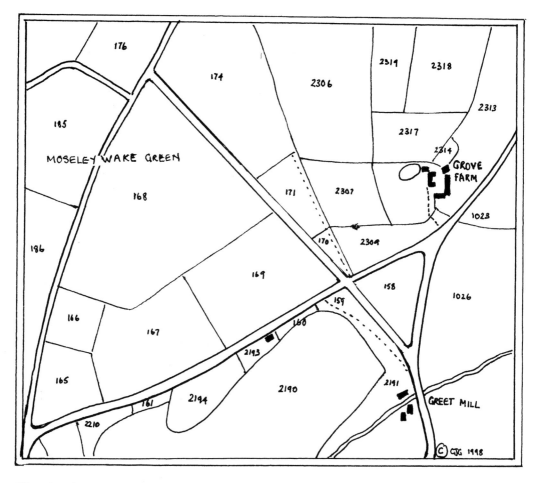

The Moseley Wake Green area prior to the building of Spring Hill College in the 1850s.
The area was dominated by Grove Farm which belonged to the Izod family. The main
network of roads can be traced from the tracks shown here.

of Worcestershire and remained largely rural. A pre-1850 map shows an
agricultural landscape with the pattern of tracks which were to become Wake
Green Road, College Road, Springfield Road and Stratford Road. The oldest
established of these was the Birmingham to Stratford Road which had operated
as a turnpike route in the previous century and which linked the only two
substantial buildings, Greet Mill and the imposing Grove Farm.

Much of the employment in the area was agricultural, although there is
evidence of the River Cole providing power for mills. The 1861 Yardley Census
recorded 77 farmers and 193 farm labourers, and 168 metal workers (many at
the BSA Works or at Webster and Horsfall at Hay Mills, and the rest working
from home). There was no tradition of large powerful landlords, however, and
most land was in the hands of small farmers or tenants, a few of whom resisted
the urbanisation of the area until the 1920s.

Grove Farm, Sparkhill, between 1850 and 1900

The influx of new inhabitants into the Parish of Yardley led to the development of improved housing for skilled craftsmen along the Stratford Road through Sparkbrook and Sparkhill, and to the establishment of Moseley as a largely middle class residential suburb. The building boom was quickly under way; by 1874 six brick and tile makers were listed in the Yardley Parish. The Sparkhill houses were a major improvement on the courts of back-to-back and tunnel-back homes in the city centre; they were mostly through houses, often with back gardens and individual toilets.

By the 1870s better-paid working class families were moving out of the overcrowded city centre into terraced housing in Sparkbrook and Sparkhill. These were mainly tunnel-back houses opening onto the street, built with outside toilets.

Through the late 1880s and 1890s more spacious houses were built in Sparkhill with bay windows and small front gardens. Still relatively few had inside toilets.

Some terraced homes were built in Moseley, usually of fairly generous proportions, but most were individually designed detached houses with large gardens. Horse omnibuses ran from Moseley to town every 15 minutes, while Sparkhill had to wait until the 1880s for steam trams to link it to the centre of Birmingham. The Gloucester railway line had been cut through Moseley Ridge and in 1867 a station was built between the Queen's bridge and the Wood bridge.

Moseley began to develop as a residential suburb from about 1870 onwards with the building of detached middle-class homes. Kelly's Directory lists 133 residents of Moseley in 1874.

Educational provision was very limited in the Yardley Parish and not much better in the Borough of Birmingham. In 1851, the Birmingham Education Society carried out an Enquiry into the city's schools, which showed that only 35 per cent of children were attending any sort of day school. Of these about half were in private schools of often dubious quality and half were in elementary schools run mainly by the Church of England on the monitorial system with few qualified teachers. Many of these schools were under-subscribed; the Enquiry found that boys spent on average less than two years in school and girls only slightly more. Poverty was one of many reasons for this and the Society set up a fund to pay the school fees of 6,000 poor children. There were a few free schools in the worst slum areas and Sunday Schools did teach some children, and some adults, to read.

Attempts to provide adult education were usually short-lived, though several important institutions of higher education were established. They included Queen's College for the training of medical students (1828), St Mary's Roman Catholic College at Oscott (1835), St Peter's Anglican teacher training college at Saltley (1852) and the Birmingham and Midland Institute (1855). The main contribution of the Protestant Nonconformists was the creation of Spring Hill College for the training of ministers, founded in 1838 and located at Wake Green from 1857.

The Birmingham Education Society grew into the National Education League, a radical organisation campaigning for free, compulsory, nonsectarian schools run by local authorities for every child in the country. The League brought together a remarkable group of Nonconformist Liberals who articulated what became known as the 'civic gospel', which was bent on making Birmingham 'a very metropolis of liberty, education and courageous municipal government'. The impetus came originally from the Rev. George Dawson, a down to earth and charismatic preacher who called for the city to make proper provision of schools, libraries, art galleries and parks as well as prisons, sewers and asylums. His style and beliefs were continued by Dr Robert W. Dale, the minister of Carr's Lane Congregational Chapel, who trained at Spring Hill College and subsequently managed it.

The most passionate educationalist in the group was George Dixon, who served as Mayor and as Member of Parliament for Birmingham for over 20 years, and who has been described as 'one of Birmingham's greatest citizens'. The most famous was Joseph Chamberlain, who combined business success with a strong sense of public duty, serving as Mayor for an unprecedented three years and as one of Birmingham's Members of Parliament for nearly 40 years. Under his leadership, a remarkable programme of civic advancement was undertaken, including the building of the Victoria Law Courts and the Council House, the purchase of the Elan Valley to create a water supply, and large scale slum clearance and housing improvements.

The members of the National Education League were disappointed that the 1870 Education Act did not do everything they had campaigned for. But it did set up the School Board system to ensure that there was a school place for every child, and enabled energetic cities to undertake pioneering developments in education. Dale, Dixon and Chamberlain all served on the Birmingham School Board (Dixon for 26 years). In its first decade, the Board built 28 Board Schools for around 1,000 children each, attendance was made compulsory by local bye-law enforced by a team of 17 attendance officers, and fees were reduced to 1d per week. The Board went on to organise teacher training and kindergartens, provide free school meals, health care and tarred playgrounds, and make arrangements for backward and delicate children. It was said that 'the Birmingham School Board led the country in its energy and organisation'; certainly the social and educational landscape of the city was radically changed.

*The Borough of Birmingham and surrounding
parishes in the middle of the last century.*

    In the less populated parishes of Greater Birmingham, change came more slowly. The Yardley School Board did not establish its first school until the 1890s; College Road Board School, the subject of Chapter 3, was thus one of its earliest ventures. From around that time, Worcestershire made great strides in its educational provision, as if to catch up with its bigger neighbour and it actually led the way in the provision of secondary schools for a time. Yardley was one of several areas to be added to the city of Birmingham in 1911, increasing its population to 850,000 and turning it into the second city in England.

References and acknowledgements

Reference has been made to C. Gill and A. Briggs, History of Birmingham (2 volumes) (1952); V. Skipp, The Making of Victorian Birmingham (1983); C. Chinn, Birmingham – The Great Working City (1996) and M. Baxter and P. Drake, Moseley, Balsall Heath and Highgate (1996). Our thanks to Richard Trengrouse for the loan of early maps.

Chapter One

Spring Hill College 1857-1886

Spring Hill College owed its foundation to one remarkable family. George Storer Mansfield, Elizabeth Mansfield and Sarah Glover (nee Mansfield) possessed both the vision and the wealth to turn a hopeful idea into a solid and impressive reality. Their wealth was inherited; their vision was shaped by the religious and social community which they joined in their adopted home, Birmingham. The combination of the two enabled the Mansfields to bring about what one contemporary described as 'one of the greatest proofs of private and public liberality in existence: begun in a small way, Spring Hill College has become one of the most important establishments for educational purposes in or around Birmingham'.

Birmingham's leading citizens were predominantly religious Nonconformists or Dissenters – Quakers, Congregationalists, Unitarians, Baptists, Methodists – at a time when Anglicans still enjoyed certain privileges associated with being the established Church. In particular, Oxford and Cambridge Universities, which were then essentially training establishments for Anglican priests, required students to subscribe to the doctrine of the Church of England. Unable to do this, Nonconformists had developed their own schools, known as Dissenting Academies which, with their broad curriculum including science and English rather than Latin, were the best educational institutions in England.

Nonconformists were typically well-educated, industrious people who were often successful in business. Their faith, centring around various chapels, was practical and philanthropic, expecting them to share responsibility for the welfare of their fellow citizens – to found and fund orphanages, hospitals, schools. Nearly all of Birmingham's successful industrialists were Nonconformists, whose religious principles guided them to donate liberally to good causes; it has been observed that 'charity was habitual enough among the wealthy for it to have been actively expected of them'. By the standards of the times, they were often enlightened employers, concerned with keeping their factories clean and smart and giving their workers holidays, education and housing. They often married within their sects, giving rise to dynasties – Cadbury, Lloyd, Ryland, Kenrick, Martineau, Chamberlain – the members of which combined successful business careers with lifetimes of public service to Birmingham.

The coming together of these two factors – the urgent need for organisation and development at a civic level and the presence of a capable and committed group of idealists – transformed Birmingham during the course of the nineteenth century. The foundation of Spring Hill College was one of the earlier and more substantial expressions of Nonconformist philanthropy. Its successful half century in Birmingham kept it involved with many of the wealthy and influential people who met at chapel on Sundays, taught Sunday school together, and planned and raised money for endless worthwhile projects.

The Mansfield family, owners of land in Leicestershire and Derbyshire, moved to a large house in Spring Hill, Birmingham in about 1803 following Sarah's marriage to Charles Glover. They met while she was staying with a friend in Tutbury, near Burton-on-Trent, while he, as one of the Guardians of the Poor in Birmingham, was visiting the Birmingham pauper children sent to work in the cotton mill there. Charles Glover (1753-1821) was a successful builder and devout Christian, who assembled his workmen for prayers every morning and refused to do business on Sundays. On the occasion of his marriage he gave the bellringers a Bible each instead of the customary ale or money! Sarah Glover (nee Mansfield) (1767-1853) was an extrovert, cheerful character who, during her long life, became renowned for her generosity to good causes of all kinds in Birmingham and beyond.

Mrs Sarah Glover, the driving force behind Spring Hill College, from a portrait now hanging in Mansfield College, Oxford.

The Glovers were joined at Spring Hill by other members of Sarah's family. Her sister, Elizabeth (1772-1847) was a shy, retiring person, of whom it was said 'no one ever lived less covetous of the applause of the world'. As a child preoccupied with a sense of sin, she grew up to become a tireless worker for the church and a very generous benefactor. Once the extended family was settled in at Spring Hill, Charles Glover converted the laundry into a little chapel and helped to build the Independent Ebenezer Chapel in Steelhouse Lane, where his wife worshipped and which he himself joined towards the end of his life. George Storer Mansfield (1764-1837) joined his sisters at Spring Hill in 1824. A shy, nervous man, he had lived much of his life in Leicestershire on his inherited estates where, it was assumed, he was 'too much addicted to such worldly pleasures as a country life affords to a gentleman of good landed property'. But he soon joined in the daily prayers and regular attendance at Ebenezer Chapel, and one of his few friends was the pastor, the Rev. Timothy East, whose advice prompted the earliest planning of Spring Hill College.

Quite late in his life, George discussed with the Rev. East, how he could use his wealth for a worthwhile purpose. 'He felt an anxious desire to do something in the way of glorifying God with that property which had hitherto been employed only for his own comfort and amusement'. Rev. East suggested the idea of a college to educate and train young men for the Christian ministry. Before his death at Spring Hill, George gave some of his land to a trust to support the college. Elizabeth and Sarah were actively involved from the start and gave generously from their own fortunes. In 1838, anxious to get the college under way, they 'with the most praiseworthy self-sacrifice' handed over their own home in Spring Hill Road and moved to a smaller residence.

The management of the proposed college was speedily organised. The Rev. East was Chairman and Treasurer, the Rev. John Angell James became Educational Chairman, and five distinguished clerical Visitors and Examiners were appointed from around the country – Stroud, Derby, Nottingham, Liverpool and Worcester. A committee of local supporters – who all had to affirm their religious belief – was formed, drawing on clergymen and laymen from Birmingham and other Midland towns, such as Dudley, Walsall, Stafford, Wolverhampton, Kidderminster and Coventry. The college was expected to serve as the Midlands centre for Nonconformity and complement the ten or so other similar establishments in different parts of England.

The College was formally opened on 2 and 3 October 1838, with addresses delivered by two of the country's foremost Nonconformist preachers. Teaching was in the hands of three tutors. The Resident Tutor (until his death in 1870) was the Rev. Thomas Barker, Professor of Languages, whose lifelong interest in Hebrew probably exceeded that of most of his students, who found him rather distant. The Rev. Francis Watts was Professor of Theology and Ecclesiastical History; his kindly but painstaking approach bored the students and led to disorder and protests. Henry Rogers, Professor of Mathematics, Philosophy and Logic was the most popular tutor; a brilliant, witty man with wide cultural interests, he encouraged lively philosophical debates and himself wrote books challenging the religious views of others.

Nine young men – from Birmingham, Hanley, Coventry, Watford, Caermarthen and Greenock – were admitted at once, and they were soon joined by four more – from Watford, Wells, Woburn and Portsea. Originally, eligible candidates for admission had to be eighteen years old and to remain for four years' theological study after a three month probationary period. But quite soon it was decided to admit lay students, boys over 16 who wished to pursue a higher education without necessarily becoming ministers. Accommodation was secured in a row of six cottages on the other side of the road, and a number of scholarships were endowed by individuals to assist needy students, including one to support missionary work. In 1840, the College took an important step in validating its academic work by affiliating to the University of London so that its students could gain degrees. London University had been recently formed, in 1838, from two earlier institutions, the Anglican King's College and non-denominational University College, and specialised in awarding degrees without a residential requirement.

The students spent much of their time studying – there was a good library – though Spring Hill students were expected to mix in the everyday world rather than be shut up as if in a monastery, and especially to attend and work in chapels around the town. For this reason, the College never had its own chapel. Robert Dale, who was subsequently to become so well-known and so closely identified with Spring Hill, arrived as an 18-year-old in 1847 and described student life thus:

> *Upon coming to the College, I was, as all juniors are, put into one room which was to serve as my study and bedroom; the said room being without a carpet, without table, having in it a high deal desk and stool to match, a reed-bottomed chair, a deal chest of drawers, and a small press (?brass) bedstead ... We are rung up at six o'clock in the morning all the year round, and generally have one class to attend before breakfast two or three times a week. The interval between breakfast and dinner at 2-30 is occupied by sundry lectures and classes; between 2-30 and 5-30 by various classes and private study. After tea, till prayers at 9, of course we have to work privately, and though the rule is a dead letter, we are required to extinguish fire and candle at 10-30.*

In that same year, the second of the original founders, Elizabeth Mansfield, died at the age of 74; tributes were paid to her 'simplicity, humility, gentleness, meekness, and patience'.

Soon after its opening, a fund was started to build a worthy home for Spring Hill College. Several large donations – an anonymous gift of £5,000, £2,000 from the Mansfield sisters, £500 each from the Rev. East, the Carr's Lane

Congregational Chapel in honour of the Rev. James, three Worcester residents – and dozens of small ones helped to swell the building fund, which was wisely invested. The chosen site was 22 acres of land acquired for £2,000 from the Yardley Inclosure Commissioners, on a 'beautiful and picturesque site on Moseley Common, commanding a fine and extensive prospect of the surrounding

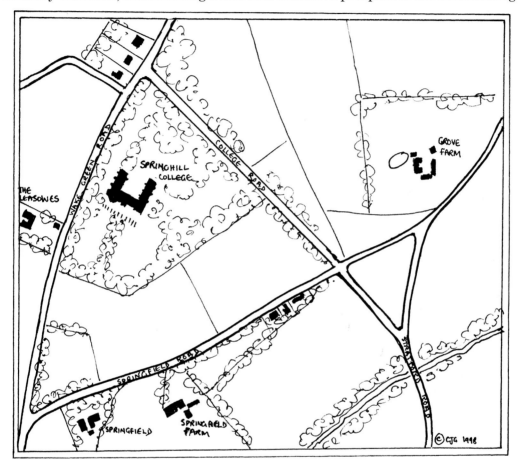

The original location of Spring Hill College became heavily industrialised. The Moseley Wake Green site was chosen for its healthy environment and also perhaps for the absence of unsuitable distractions for its students.
The area was still mainly rural, although the roads now had names; a few large houses had been built by the 1880s.

country'. And country it was. Moseley was then a hamlet, three miles from the centre of Birmingham, and the names we now associate with busy city life in South Birmingham are all reminders of its rural origins: 'heath', 'hill', 'brook', 'green', 'common', 'wood'. As the character of the original Spring Hill location changed – 'from the rapid increase of manufactories around it, it was becoming disagreeable', with an ironworks on one side and chemical works on the other – the move to a more congenial and healthy location became urgent.

Apart from a few large private houses, the College's only neighbours were the Moseley Quoit and Bowling Club in College Road, whose members are shown here in the mid 1870s.

The organising committee set about raising the £10,000 it thought it would need. The committee was determined to raise sufficient money to do the job properly, and the choices it made in its planning of the new building are all evidence of the high status which Spring Hill College, Wake Green, Moseley, was intended to have. As the plans took shape and costs rose towards the £18,000 which the new building eventually totalled, funds were solicited from all possible sources of support – large sums from a few wealthy patrons and an appeal for collections 'however small' in chapels all over the Midlands. Between 1854 and 1857 well over a hundred separate donations of over £10 each were received, with some considerably larger. Birmingham itself accounted for about half the donors; the rest were from individuals and chapels in many parts of the country, including Leicester, Coventry, Nottingham, Manchester and Bristol.

Advertisements in the 'Builder' newspaper invited designs, with prizes of £100 and £50 for the best two, and from twenty-five entries, a shortlist of six was drawn up. The committee meeting to choose the winner was the very day of the funeral of the last of the original founders, Mrs Sarah Glover, who died at the age of 86 'full of years and of honours'. She thus never saw the college 'to which she had looked forward with such untiring anxiety and hope for many years'. The chosen design was by Joseph James of London, a 25-year-old architect, possibly a nephew of the Rev. Angell James, who in his relatively short life (1828-1875) was to become the leading Congregational church architect of his generation.

The south front of Spring Hill College shown in an early engraving.

The building contract was awarded to George Myers, who had a national reputation as a builder, mason and furniture-maker and worked for some of the most famous designers of the nineteenth century, including Pugin and William Morris. The unusually high quality of some of the details and joinery

Much of the decorative stone work, such as this buttress to the right of the tower,
was the work of the builder – George Myers of London.

Myers was also responsible for the high quality detail as in the carving of the rainwater spouts and the design of the cast iron rainwater goods.

and the intricate carving of imported French stone, are attributable to him. The specially designed stained glass was commissioned from the Nonconformist firm of Messrs. Chance of Smethwick, the leading glass manufacturer in the country, which had recently supplied nearly a million feet of window glass for the construction of London's famous Crystal Palace in 1851.

Building work began in 1854, and the new College opened on 24 June 1857. It was a remarkable building. Nonconformists often preferred a rather plain,

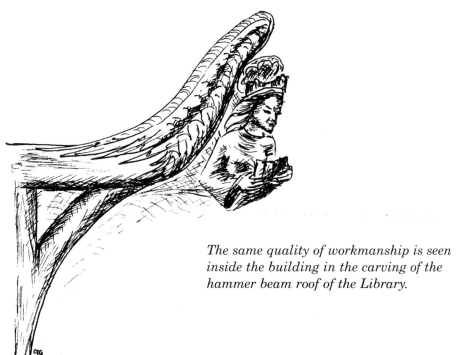

The same quality of workmanship is seen inside the building in the carving of the hammer beam roof of the Library.

functional style of architecture, believing that God did not favour the lavish ornamentation associated with High Church religion. But Birmingham had developed its own 'Gothic' style of architecture, for which it became notable, and Spring Hill College was clearly intended to be a particularly impressive version of that style, to emphasise the importance of the institution.

The wonderful contemporary description of the College which appeared in Dr Langford's Handbook is reproduced here. But in brief, the two-storey

"The style is that of the early part of the fifteenth century, the details inclining more to the decorated period than to the perpendicular. The building forms three sides of a quadrangle, the main front being to the south. In the centre of the south front is a battlemented tower, 78 feet in height, flanked by a bell turret carried 14 feet higher. In this tower is the principal entrance to the building. The doorway is exceedingly beautiful, the carving with which the face of the arch is enriched being a clever combination of many of the best examples, all brought out with scrupulous care. One of the bands bears the inscription, 'The fear of the Lord is the beginning of wisdom'; and on each side are shields, on which are inscribed, 'On earth peace, goodwill to men,' and 'Glory to God in the highest.' Above the main entrance rise, in succession, three bay windows, for the lighting respectively of Council room, museum, and laboratory. The tracery of these windows is of a very elaborate character, a buttress to the right of the doorway being decidedly original and beautiful in form. To the west of the tower is the library, on the exterior of which a large amount of ornament has been lavished. It is lighted by four very large moulded windows of stained glass, supplied by Messrs. Chance, of Spon Lane. Over the tracery is a rich pierced parapet, surmounted by four elegantly-carved pinnacles. Immediately beyond the library, and forming the west angle, is the Warden's house, flanked by an octagon turret, on the summit of which is a water tank for the use of the establishment. To the east of the tower is the dining hall, with lecture room over it; and beyond these the matron's residence. The wings, which are two-storied and have transomed windows, are in keeping with the main front, though not so rich in decoration. At the end of each turret is a bell turret. Inside is a handsome entrance hall, paved with encaustic tiles, and having in one of the walls a most elaborate piece of carving, in Caen stone, intended to serve as a frame for a metallic tablet to be erected to the memory of the original founders of Spring Hill College, Mr. G.S. Mansfield, Mr. Charles Glover, Mrs. Sarah Glover, and Miss Elizabeth Mansfield. A corridor window, immediately fronting the entrance hall, is fitted with stained glass and contains the Mansfield and Glover arms, together with those of the three county towns, Warwick, Worcester, and Stafford. The library, the entrance to which is from the hall, is a fine, lofty apartment, open roofed, the principals resting on corbels of winged angels. Bookshelves are carried round three sides of the room, and over these is a small gallery. As regards detail, the most noteworthy feature of the library is the chimney-piece at either end. Both are of Caen stone; they have the appropriate motto, 'Scientia potentia est'; and they are covered with the most delicate carving which human hand sever executed. Each flower or bit of foliage introduced is worthy of special study. Imagine a lily-of-the-valley, for instance, executed in high relief, with nearly as much delicacy as nature's self could give it. The carver could not have been more successful if wax or Parian marble had been his material, instead of stone dug out of the quarries of Normandy. One chimney-piece is surmounted by a bust of Dr. Joseph Fletcher, formerly of Stepney, the other by a bust of Dr. Pye Smith, who may, we suppose, be regarded as the "representative man" of Nonconforming collegiate life. The dining-room has also two fine chimney-pieces, more massive in style, but with carving equally beautiful. None of the other public rooms call for special remark. Along the north side of the principal building runs a lengthy corridor, with pointed arches, the perspective effect of which is a very fine one. The wings are appropriated to the students; the studies being on the first floor, and the dormitories overhead. Each study has an area ten feet by eleven feet, and is nine feet in height. There is at present accommodation for thirty-six students; but at the cost of a couple of thousand pounds this could be easily doubled by running a centre building into te quadrangle. The kitchens, etc., are in the basement story of the east wing. All the internal arrangements seem complete, and not the least satisfactory is the apparatus which heats the building."

building, of red brick with extensive stonework around the windows and doors, was fifteenth century in style. It formed three sides of a quadrangle, with cloisters giving on to the semi-enclosed courtyard. The front faced south and was dominated by a four-storey tower in the centre, which housed the impressive main entrance. To the west of the tower was the library, a large and lofty room with fine windows and chimney-pieces, which was also used for meetings and services. To the east was the dining hall with a lecture room on the first floor. The east and west wings both housed accommodation for thirty-six students in

EAST ELEVATION OF EAST WING

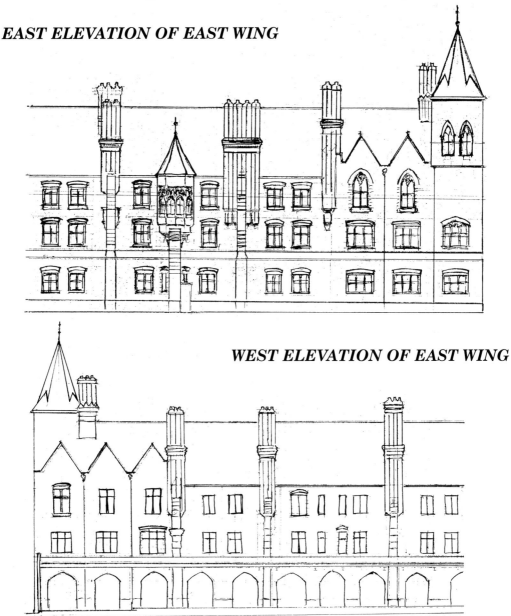

WEST ELEVATION OF EAST WING

The only elevation drawings of the original building; they show clearly the decorative chimneys and turret and the original line of cloister-like arches before building work altered the ground level and partially obscured them.

all – studies on the ground floor and bedrooms above – though the west wing was much more decorated externally. It ran parallel to what became Wake Green Road, with the main approach being to the back of the west wing. The two front corners of the building were devoted to residential accommodation: the very elegant Principal's house to the west and the plainer matron's house to the east.

Spring Hill College as shown in the Congregational Year Book of 1858.

It is not clear how the grounds were landscaped. Early illustrations show a very open aspect and it is probable that the heavy tree-planting occurred at a later date, in its life as a botanical garden. But the imposing avenue of horse chestnut trees which ran right down the field in front of the main entrance may well have been planted earlier, as a fitting approach to 'the Obelisk'. This was a substantial stone monument engraved *Dux femina facti*, meaning 'a woman was leader of the action' and was presumably erected by the Spring Hill trustees as a tribute to the founding sisters. It impressed schoolboys in the 1920s, until its removal to Mansfield College, Oxford.

It is worth remembering that large buildings were rare in the nineteenth century landscape. The neighbourhood around the College was scarcely developed at all, and even in the city itself there was just a handful of substantial public buildings: the recently completed Town Hall, the brand new Midland Institute, the huge Workhouse at Winson Green, Queen's College medical school and half a dozen parish churches. Most of Birmingham's Victorian heritage – the Central Library, the Council House, Mason's Science College (the original University of Birmingham), the General Hospital, the Museum and Art Gallery, the Victoria Law Courts – was yet to be constructed.

Of a number of substantial buildings erected for similar purposes in and around Birmingham in the mid-nineteenth century, such as the Anglican St. Peter's College at Saltley and Oscott Roman Catholic College, Spring Hill College has been judged to be the most architecturally successful. One expert rates it more highly than almost all the public schools and Oxford and Cambridge colleges built around that time. It is a particularly significant expression of the material and spiritual self-confidence of the Nonconformist community at its zenith.

The opening of the new College building coincided with changes in personnel, as Professors Rogers and Watts both moved on. The Rev. Dr Alliott, a Glasgow University graduate and tutor at another Nonconformist academy, Cheshunt College, was appointed as the new Principal, even though the Rev. Barker was still in post, and the Rev. Henry Goward M.A., LL.B. (a recent Spring Hill graduate) became assistant tutor. There was great sadness at the death of one of the College's staunchest supporters, the Rev. Angell James, after twenty years as the educational chairman and forty years as Minister of Carr's Lane Congregational Chapel. He was succeeded in both posts by one of Spring Hill's most distinguished former students, the Rev. Robert Dale. Most of the Rev. James' valuable collection of books was donated by his son to the Spring Hill College Library.

There were two distinct courses offered by the College – the four-year Theological course for advanced students from age 18, and the General course, from age 16, lasting up to five years if a London B.A. and M.A. were obtained. The College year started in September, and applicants had to be recommended by at least one minister, to furnish a medical certificate, to undergo an interview and examination, and to declare in writing that they were Dissenters from the Established Church. Ministers furnishing testimonials were requested to respond to a number of specific questions, including:

Is the candidate a young man of serious and fervent piety?

Is his character without reproach?

Is he amiable in his disposition, temper, and deportment? Or has he shown a conscientious desire to correct what is amiss?

Has he manifested a personal devotedness to the cause of Christ, and a concern for the instruction of the ignorant, and the salvation of souls? – such as the distribution of tracts, Sabbath school instruction, or visits to the poor.

Has he manifested any symptoms of unsound or feeble health?

Is he free from all peculiarity of voice or utterance?

A review of the College's achievements in 1860 shows that there were then 20 students in residence, all but one of them in receipt of some kind of scholarship, and they came from all over the country, including Scotland and Wales. By that time, Spring Hill students were regularly gaining success in London University's B.A. and M.A. examinations. For the senior students, there were Biblical Studies and Theology, Latin and Greek, Mathematics and English Literature. The junior class, with a more varied educational background before they came to Spring Hill, studied similar subjects at a simpler level, along with English Grammar and, for a while, Chemistry.

By 1860, a total of 66 young men had passed through Spring Hill College; 37 took degrees, of whom 27 were working as ministers; 29 were 'Non-University Men', of whom 18 were ministers; two had died and a further 12 had not completed the course because of illness or 'some other unfitness for the ministry'. The College proudly recorded those of its students who had subsequently been ordained, noting that they served chapels in over 30 towns throughout Britain, as well as Bangalore, Sydney and British Columbia. It was a remarkable record, leading one contemporary to applaud 'the brilliant band of men who won no little reputation in the land for what was then relatively a small theological college.'

The lives of the students probably continued much as before: lectures, classes, private study and religious observance relieved by periods of relaxation and leisure. An early and most welcome gift had been the provision of an 'excellent gymnasium' by a supporter in Wolverhampton which, it was hoped, would encourage the students to 'take that exercise which is so essential to the preservation of their health and to the vigour of their minds'. Local residents in Hall Green and Yardley Wood used to recall meeting happy groups of students from 'the College' walking in the country lanes on sunny afternoons.

The approach to Spring Hill College in the 1860s was from the junction of Wake Green Road and College Road. The turrets at the near end of each wing were removed in the 1920s during the conversion to a school building.

Another happy recollection concerned the meeting and subsequent marriage between a Spring Hill student, Edwin Simon, and Fanny Allsebrook, the sister of his friend and fellow student; their son John was to become the first Viscount Simon, having achieved high government office in the 1930s.

Despite their pious calling, Spring Hill students were not always as well behaved as their tutors would have wished. In 1862, Principal Barker spoke of the 'fearful amount of crime, immorality, vice and profanity' which he had discovered in the College and five students were charged with irreverent behaviour and loose conversation. Three were subsequently expelled, though there was such an outcry that they were reinstated.

The College's sojourn in Moseley was also plagued by staffing difficulties. Dr Alliott and his successor, the Rev. Bubier, both died after short tenures of office, and in 1869, Spring Hill acquired a new Principal, David Worthington Simon. Simon was a fine theologian and a challenging and interesting teacher, but was thought by some Congregationalists to be rather unorthodox and to encourage his students to be too questioning. After difficulties with his health and an extended absence, he moved to a post in Scotland in 1883. His replacement, Dr George Deane, who was a scientist of some repute, resigned in 1884. With several changes in the assistant tutors as well, it contributed to this being a period when 'changes and uncertainties in connection with the professional staff had an unfavourable influence on the work and fortunes of the College'.

It must have been extremely disappointing for those who had worked so hard to establish the College at Moseley that it failed to attract a settled staff, or to prosper more conspicuously during this period. The reason may be connected to the external challenges described below, which obliged Nonconformists to re-consider several aspects of their faith and prompted some of them, including the Congregationalists, to move towards greater orthodoxy.

During the 1870s, Spring Hill was caught up in the debate about the future of Nonconformist education which followed the abolition of almost all the religious tests at Oxford and Cambridge Universities after decades of bitter argument. At last Nonconformists could study and obtain degrees at England's premier centres of learning. As young men increasingly took advantage of the opportunity so long denied to them, the senior members of their sects agonised over the best way forward for Nonconformist higher education. Some felt that Oxford and Cambridge colleges, patronised by the rich and privileged, were an unsuitable moral environment for young Nonconformists, who found it difficult to withdraw from the customary attendance at Anglican services in their college chapels. Others believed that it was all the more important to establish a Nonconformist centre there, both to support their own students and to ensure that their ministers were educated to the highest standards.

Oxford seemed to be more interested than Cambridge. Senior Oxford dons such as T.H. Green and Benjamin Jowett, who were of a tolerant persuasion, lent their support and found a willing listener in Robert Dale of Spring Hill College. Dale had even received personal encouragement from Prime Minister

Gladstone, and he determined that Spring Hill should be the institution from which the new Oxford college would grow. He then spent five difficult years winning over his fellow Congregationalists and sorting out the details and technicalities associated with moving out of Spring Hill College, Birmingham and into Mansfield College, Oxford. The College was to have a new Principal. This opened the way for the appointment of Andrew Martin Fairbairn, a distinguished scholar who was then Principal of Airedale College, the Congregational college in Bradford; he and Dale have been described as 'the two finest Congregational theologians of the century'.

The remarkable stature of Robert Dale (1829-1895) deserves a little more attention. A Londoner who came to study at Spring Hill College as a young man, he was intimately involved with it for the whole time it was at Moseley. He succeeded the Rev. Angell James as Educational Chairman of the College and as minister at Carr's Lane Chapel, where he began a career which was to make him one of the most famous preachers of his generation; it is said that he was simply known as 'Dale of Birmingham' all over the world. As well as being a distinguished theologian, two passionate beliefs dominated his thinking. Firstly, he dismissed the idea that ministers were superior to their congregations, refusing to wear clerical clothes or be addressed as 'Reverend'. He was genuinely interested in the lives of ordinary working people, became knowledgeable about industrial and commercial matters, and thought that 'the skilled artisan of Birmingham was the best hearer he had ever found.'

Secondly, Robert Dale saw no distinction between religion and politics – true Christians should work to make people's lives better. He was actively involved with the Liberal Party in shaping the new civic spirit which 'was bent on making Birmingham a very metropolis of liberty, education, and courageous municipal government'. He had a particular interest in education (his own chapel ran Sunday schools for over a thousand children) and worked with leading figures in Birmingham, such as George Dixon, Joseph Chamberlain and the charismatic preacher George Dawson, to create the National Education League campaigning for universal compulsory secular education. Despite their disappointment that the 1870 Act stopped short of such a radical reform, they all served on the Birmingham School Board; Dale was involved for its crucial first ten years when 28 board schools for 1,000 children each were built. The political dimension to Dale's beliefs and work can be said to have linked Spring Hill intimately with the nineteenth century transformation of Birmingham, which made it 'quite simply, the best governed city in the world'.

Back in Oxford, land was bought from Merton College, though Mansfield College did not wait for its new building and began in temporary premises in October 1886. The character of the institution was somewhat changed, so that it offered a post-graduate, non-residential theological training for the ministry. Six Spring Hill students were thought good enough to study at Mansfield, five transferred to other provincial colleges and one left. Dale, Fairbairn and others toured endlessly around the country raising nearly £50,000 to fund the new

Mansfield College, Oxford.

college, which opened ceremonially in October 1889 in a building rather plainer than Spring Hill, though not unattractive. The Spring Hill Trust Fund remained in existence for many years, and some money was expected to be raised by the sale of the Spring Hill College building in Wake Green, Moseley, though it must have been difficult to imagine, at that point, to what alternative use the unique building could be put.

References and acknowledgements

This chapter has been compiled from many sources, notably G. Griffiths, History of the Free-Schools, Colleges, Hospitals, and Asylums Of Birmingham (1861); R.K. Dent, Old and New Birmingham (1880) & The Making of Birmingham (1894); J.H. Muirhead, Nine Famous Birmingham Men (1909); and E. Kay, Mansfield College, Oxford (1996); with additional background information from The Birmingham Red Book (various years 1860s-1890s); Kelly's and other Directories (various years); C. Gill & A. Briggs, History of Birmingham (2 vols) (1952); J. Zuckerman & G. Eley, Birmingham Heritage (1979); V. Skipp, The Making of Victorian Birmingham (1983); and C. Upton, A History of Birmingham (1993); The Congregational Year Book (1958); and the Local Studies section of the Birmingham Central Library. Our thanks to Roy Holloway for help with the Mansfield College research.

Chapter Two

The Pine Dell Hydropathic Establishment and Moseley Botanical Gardens 1886-1900 and the War Years 1914-1922

The Nonconformist founders of Spring Hill College probably did not envisage that its next incarnation would be a Victorian health establishment and pleasure garden. Following the removal of Spring Hill College to Mansfield College in 1886, the building remained empty until 1892 when it was purchased by Mr William Ross. Little is known about him, except that he may have been a trustee of the College and that he was probably a builder by occupation. His plans for the site were ambitious; he invested in new construction and re-opened it as the Pine Dell Hydropathic Establishment with the grounds restyled as Moseley Botanical Gardens. This fashionable venture must have been particularly harmonious with the surrounding area. 'Moseley's green uplands' notes an old newspaper article 'became one of the favourite settling-places for monied

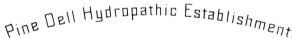

Swimming Baths.
Droitwich Brine,
Turkish,
Russian,
and full set of
Hydropathic Baths
also Massage
& Baths of Various kinds.

Over 20 Acres of
Beautifully Wooded
Grounds,
Lawn Tennis.

Moseley Station M.R.
The Omnibuses
of the Establishment
meet Trains when required

500 FEET ABOVE THE SEA LEVEL

MOSELEY WAKE GREEN,
NEAR BIRMINGHAM.

A contemporary advertisement.

men in Victorian times', with 'ample and handsome houses', spacious croquet lawns and 'smart riders' promenading on horseback.

Several additions were made to the site by William Ross, financed by the sale of plots of land on College Road for the building of terraced housing. A number of Ross family members appear to have moved into the new houses, among them a Miss Annie Ross and Harry Ross at different addresses. To create Pine Dell, a large glass-roofed building was erected on the eastern side of what had been the cloistered quadrangle of the College to house a swimming bath and bath houses – later to become the School Assembly Hall. A well was

All that can be seen of the bath house today.
The floor of the assembly hall above was laid in the late 1920s during the conversion to school buildings.

sunk east of the east wing to ensure a sufficient supply of water for the baths and laundry. This was a very substantial structure, with a subterranean dome-shaped housing containing a walkway surround and a fireplace, presumably to heat the water. The water from the well was 'noted for its purity and healing qualities', but also 'for the fact that no matter how hot the day the water was never more than three degrees above freezing'. Later excavation of the well found a tunnel running back to the main building, whose purpose remains somewhat mysterious. A complete central heating system was installed, its

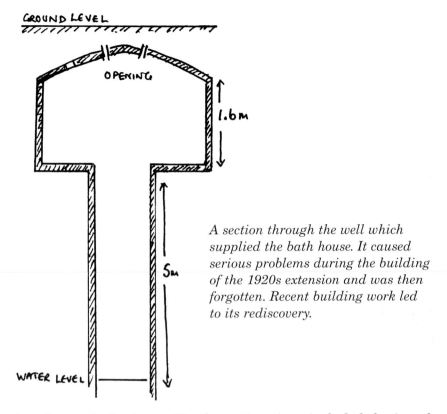

GROUND LEVEL

OPENING

1.6m

5m

WATER LEVEL

A section through the well which supplied the bath house. It caused serious problems during the building of the 1920s extension and was then forgotten. Recent building work led to its rediscovery.

boilers located underneath the tower. Further attractions included the installation of a picture gallery in the lower corridor and Turkish Baths, probably located in the rooms now occupied by the gym. The grounds, over 20 acres in extent, were restored and landscaped.

Pine Dell advertised its attractions for 'resident visitors' from five shillings per day, seven shillings if full Hydropathic Treatment was included. Non-residents could purchase up to thirty different kinds of baths and treatments. Hydropathy 'in all its forms' noted the advertisements, 'is administered by experienced attendants'. The publicity added 'There is scarcely a disease where Hydropathy does not give relief or cure' and, curiously, 'Outdoor treatment administered'. Prominent in the advertisements was Wake Green's elevated and healthy atmosphere: '500 feet above the sea level' was emblazoned beneath the title.

The swimming bath was open to the public every day of the week from 6 a.m. until 9 p.m. and on Sunday until 10 p.m. Special times were set aside for ladies only swimming and ladies' use of the Turkish Baths. Discounts were offered for parties or bulk purchase: six 2/- tickets were issued for 10/6 and twelve for 20/- or £1. The Gardens alone could be entered with a sixpenny ticket, later increased to ninepence. Transport from Moseley Station was provided: 'the Omnibuses of the Establishment meet Trains when required' declared the advertisement.

The menu of hydropathic treatments combines some that we would recognise today with a number of Victorian specialities. Turkish Baths and Russian Baths,

Moseley station in the 1890s.

Sitz Baths 'in various forms' and half hour Massage sessions were offered. Reflecting the popularity of other spas, Pine Dell also offered Droitwich Brine Baths (at 3/-) and Harrogate Sulphur Baths (2/6); it claimed to transport brine from Droitwich, but the size of the establishment's well may cast some doubt on this.

Treatments which sound intriguing and which must have been, at the very least, stimulating included 'Lamp Bath with soaping and rain bath', 'Liver Bath with mustard to legs', 'Carbolic Acid Fomentation' and 'Spinal Douche'. Customers could avail themselves of 'Hot and Cold dripping Sheets' for a mere 1/6 and 'Rubbing with Chillie Paste' was offered for 6d 'after any bath', or a shilling more 'without bath'. The most expensive item was an Electric Bath for 3/6.

Pine Dell Hydropathic Establishment, Moseley.

WAKE GREEN, Nr. Birmingham.

GROUNDS OVER 20 ACRES IN EXTENT.   500 FEET ABOVE THE SEA LEVEL.

TERMS FOR RESIDENT VISITORS FROM 5/- PER DAY.

Including full Hydropathic Treatment 7/- per day.   Massage Extra.

PRICE LIST OF HYDROPATHIC AND OTHER BATHS FOR NON-RESIDENTS

Lamp Bath with soaping and rain bath	2/-	Sitz Baths in various forms	2/-	Pine Baths	2/6
Vapour ,, ,, ,,	2/-	Spinal Rubbing	2/-	Electric ,.	3/6
Liver Pack ,, ,, ,,	2/-	Spinal Douche	1/-	Harrogate Sulphur Bath	2/6
Sheet ,, ,, ,,	2/-	Hot Mustard leg Bath	2/-	Massage per half hour for Gentlemen	3/-
Fever ,, ,, ,,	2/-	Carbolic Acid Fomentation	2/6	,, ,, ,, Ladies	3/-
Liver ,, with mustard to legs	2/6	Hot and Cold dripping Sheets	1/6	Turkish Baths	2/-
Soda ,, ,,	2/-	Rubbing with Chillie Paste after any Bath 6d.		,, ,, after 6 p.m. any day	1/-
Dry ,, ,,	2/-	,, ,, ,, without Bath	1/6	Russian Bath	2/-
Fomentation Pack ,,	2/-	Droitwich Brine Baths	3/-	Russian with Turkish	3/-
		Brine Douches	2/6	Leg and Arm	1/6

HOT OR COLD BATHS.

SIX TWO SHILLING TICKETS ISSUED FOR **10/6.** TWELVE FOR **20/-.** SIX THREE SHILLING TICKETS FOR **16/-**

In addition to the above Baths, Hydropathy in all its forms is administered by experienced attendants. There is scarcely a disease where Hydropathy does not give relief or cure. Outdoor treatment administered.

THE TURKISH BATH is reserved for Ladies on Tuesdays from 8 a.m. until 6 p.m. and on Fridays from 2 till 6 p.m. Tickets issued each day until 4 p.m. all other Baths open every week-day for Ladies and Gentlemen.

THE SWIMMING BATH is open every day from 6 a.m. until 9 p.m. Sundays from 6 a.m. until 10, reserved for Ladies on Tuesdays from 8 a.m. until 5 p.m. Fridays from 2 p.m. until 9, Saturdays from 8 a.m. until 1 p.m.

MASSAGE A SPECIALITY

The gardens were 'a beautiful and impressive sight' combining cultivated and manicured areas with woodland wilderness. An avenue of 'cedar trees, said to have come from Mount Lebanon' led down the centre of what is now the school field. (The two surviving examples would indicate that they were actually chestnut trees.) Ten large greenhouses supplied fruit and vegetables and 'great flower beds' enchanted the visitor. Lawn tennis courts were a feature. The Birmingham Post greeted the opening of the Moseley Botanical Gardens in rapturous tones (10 June, 1892):

The new public gardens which were formerly Spring Hill College grounds are not only situated in one of the prettiest parts of Moseley, but are probably not excelled in beauty and diversity of scene by any estate, private or public, in the environs of Birmingham. Portions of the grounds are full of the charm of wildness, for they have been left untouched since the days when they formed part of Billesley Common; while other portions, consisting of broad lawn and well-grown forest trees (chiefly pine, fir and cedar) possess the stately character of a nobleman's park. There is also a walk of a mile and a half through rich undergrowth and beneath interlacing branches.

c1895 – Entrance to Moseley Botanical Gardens and Pine Dell Hydropathic Establishment.

From the beginning Pine Dell brought music and entertainment to its glorious setting. The Birmingham Post article continues:

> *An excellent band plays on the lawn afternoon and evening, and occasional vocal selections are given. During the holidays there is a Punch and Judy entertainment for the children.*

The Establishment rapidly developed its programme of cultural activities and entertainments, with promenade concerts, band recitals, galas and firework displays. Pine Dell was also used for important meetings and events. 'In short' notes a 1948 history in the Moseleian magazine 'the buildings became the social centre for south Birmingham'. One meeting held there produced the inauguration of the Early Closing League and in 1895 Mr (afterwards Sir) Austen Chamberlain made a speech 'the subject matter of which is, unfortunately, lost to us'.

Programme.   :   :

WEDNESDAY EVENING, JULY 21st, 1897.
7-30.

Overture	" Pique Dame "		*Suppé.*
	The Band.		
1 — *Short Piece*	" Valse a Toi "		*Waldteufel,*
	The Band.		
2 — *Song*	" When the Children are Asleep."		*Hutchinson.*
	Miss Agnes Bendall.		
3 — *Song*	" The Sailor's Grave "		*Sullivan.*
	Mr. J. W. TURNER.		
4. *Danse Espagnole*			*S. Jones.*
	The Band.		
5. —*Duet*	" The Last Milestone "		*Fontel.*
	Misses Bendall.		
6. *Song*	" The Fandolero "		*Stuart.*
	Mr. Harry Smallwood.		
7. *Grand Selection*	" La Fille Tambour Major "		*Offenbach.*
	The Band		

INTERVAL.

8. *Overture*	" Poet and Peasant "		*Suppé.*
	The Band.		
9. *Song*	" Dearie "		*Lloyd.*
	Miss Kate Bendall.		
10. *Song*	" The Children's Home "		*Cowen.*
	Mr. J. W. TURNER.		
11. *Selection*	" Shop Girl "		*Caryll.*
	The Band.		
12. —*Song*	" The Yeoman's Wedding "		*Pomatouske.*
	Mr. Harry Smallwood.		
13. *Duet*	" Ora Pro Nobis "		*Piccolomini.*
	Misses Bendall.		
14. *Galop*	" Summer Night in Denmark "		*Lumbye.*
	The Band.		

God Save the Queen.

An insight into musical tastes of the time.

Surviving concert programmes from 1893 to 1898 reveal that the orchestra would play for two hours in the afternoon, with a promenade concert starting at 7.30 p.m. At one such concert, on Saturday 9 April 1898, vocalists Miss Nellie Pritchard and Mr William Ellis entertained the crowds with songs like Princess May and the Bedouin Love Song, Mont Blanc and A May Morning, and selections from Il Trovatore. On Friday 3 June 1898, Miss Annie Wilson and Mr Musgrove Tufnail sang Love's Golden Dream, Donald, Down the Vale and a duet dubiously entitled Dat's Why the Sun am Shinin'. Selections from operas – Capricciosa, Faust and The Sultan of Mocha – were regular items, and so were solo performances on the violin, 'clarionet', bassoon, piccolo, oboe and xylophone.

Mr Ross 'has long proved himself a successful caterer of public amusements' reported the Moseley Society Journal 'but few of his efforts have been more successful and pleasing than the Maypole dances'. Easter Monday and Tuesday, 11 and 12 April 1898 promised 'Seven Hours' Continuous Entertainment' commencing each day at 3.00 p.m. Along with the orchestra and vocalists, Mr Blitz, an Illusionist, and Professor Cleals 'in his Mimical and Ventriloquial Entertainment' were on the bill. 'Albert's Punch and Judy' and the 'Battle of Confetti' were staged each evening, and a 'Cinematograph' was available on Monday evening only, at 9.30 p.m. The Battle of Confetti had become a regular feature following its introduction at Pine Dell in 1896; the Birmingham Post of 16 August in that year records this important cultural event as the first time confetti was used in England!

On 21 July 1897, the Moseley Botanical Gardens played host to a Garden Party in aid of the Sparkhill, Greet and District Ladies' Nursing Guild. The aim of the event was to raise funds – £100 to maintain the Guild annually and to 'secure to the poor permanently a Nurse, who would be indeed a real comfort to the people and helpful to the Medical Attendant'. The programme describes how the recently formed Guild came into being:

> The interest of these Ladies in Sick Nursing was aroused by their attending lectures on the subject at the Sparkhill Institute; and they felt that, even in a small degree, they might alleviate the sufferings of the sick, if they formed themselves into a guild and visited all cases of illness, when desired by the Doctors or others who knew the sufferers to be in need.

The 'Jubilee Commemoration Committee of Sparkhill' had appealed for donations 'but it is feared that the response has not been such as the necessity of the case demands. ... Mr Ross, in a most generous spirit, offered to this Committee the free use of these beautiful gardens for a day, which offer was accepted'. Mr Ross's philanthropic nature was also shown by his organisation of a 'benefit concert ... a complimentary one, for the benefit of the working-staff of the grounds', reported in the Moseley Society Journal. The programme 'was an exceedingly attractive one, and was greatly appreciated by a large and enthusiastic audience'.

The programme at the Nursing Guild's Garden Party consisted of two hours of band music in the afternoon and a concert of songs and orchestral selections in the evening. In between, 'Professor Bates' Aquatic Troupe, in the swimming bath' presented an entertainment which included the intriguing 'Drinking under water', 'Like a Dog (large Dog)', 'Sleeping on the Bottom of the Bath', 'Swimming on a Chair', 'Singing "Daisy" under water', 'Imitation of a Seal: Ditto Porpoise', 'Christian Martyr' and 'Shadow Swimming' (an early precursor of synchronised swimming?). This was followed by a Polo Match and Team Race between the Y.M.C.A. and Smethwick, and an Athletic Display by the Dolobran Ladies' and Gentlemen's Athletic Club.

PROFESSOR BATES'

AQUATIC TROUPE,

IN THE SWIMMING BATH.

Plunging—various styles: Swimming up side down; Breast Stroke, Back Stroke; Side Stroke; Over Arm Stroke; One Arm and One Leg; No Arms: Drinking under water; Swimming under water: Leap Frog: Under and Over; Like a Dog (large Dog), like a Puppy Dog: Sleeping on the Bottom of the Bath; Spinning like a Top; Swimming on a Chair; Swimming like a Crab. Swimming like a Fish; Singing "Daisy" under water: Standing on the hands under water; Ditto one hand: Walking on the hands: Pushing across the Baths; Sculling Backwards and Forwards: Imitation of a Seal: Ditto Porpoise: Diving for Plates: Shadow Swimming: Floating—various styles; Jack in the Box; Christian Martyr; FINAL Best Method Saving Life in case of Drowning.

POLO MATCH and TEAM RACE,

Y.M.C.A.　v　SMETHWICK.

Athletic Display

BY THE——

DOLOBRAN Ladies' and Gentlemen's Athletic Club.

One of the more exotic entertainments presented by the Pine Dell.

The concert programmes were heavily subsidised by advertisements, which give a fascinating glimpse into Birmingham's thriving industrial and commercial life at the end of the nineteenth century and suggest a consumer society already in full swing. All manner of products and businesses were promoted: paper hangings, bicycles, 'best house and kitchen coals', joinery, glass and china, furnishing ironmongery ('trunks, brooms, brushes, coal vases, lamps, globes – Best American Lamp Oils Delivered Free'), building supplies, 'Fine Shropshire Fed Beef and Mutton', grocery and confectionery, boots and shoes, clothes of all kinds. Hatters, glovers and collarmakers plied their wares; William Denley of Corporation Street advertised 'Ladies' Dress and Mantle Trimmings: Leading Styles at Lowest Prices: Novelties Received Daily'. T. Broadbent's business in Sparkhill offered 'Hair Cutting, Shaving and Shampooing Saloons' along with his other skills as 'Picture Frame Maker, Contractor, Carver, and Gilder, Umbrellas made, repaired and re-covered at shortest notice. Cycles sold, bought, or exchanged. All kinds of Accessories in stock'.

John J. Fitter advertised watch, clock and jewellery repairs, selling 'Grammar School Badges, Solid Silver, 10p each' and 'Ladies Silver Watches from 10/6 to £4'; his shop in Stratford Road offered 'over 1000 pairs of spectacles and eye-glasses to select from'. Several 'high class' bakers and confectioners advertised in Pine Dell's programmes; one offered 'Hovis Bread Fresh Every Day' and Horniman's and Ceylon tea, while another offered 'Bride Cakes made to order, Rich, Sultana, Currant, Seed, and Madeira Cake, and all kinds of Pastry'. A name still familiar today, R. White's of Saltley, promoted their ginger beer and high-class mineral waters, sparkling lemonade, orange quinine, 'hop ale, wiskey stout, and kops ale'.

Despite all these efforts, it is believed that the venture was not a commercial success and in 1900 William Ross closed Pine Dell Hydropathic Establishment and Moseley Botanical Gardens. The Ross family continued to live in the building as a private residence for some years.

In 1914, it was commandeered as a barracks for the 16th Battalion of the Royal Warwickshire Regiment. This Battalion was formed when Alderman W. H. Bowater, Deputy Mayor of Birmingham, proposed to Lord Kitchener in a letter dated 28 August 1914 'to raise and equip a battalion of young business men for service in His Majesty's Army'. The subsequent call for recruits of 'young men of all grades of society engaged in non-manual occupations' attracted 4,500 in

HEADQUARTERS, 3RD CITY BATTALION,
THE COLLEGE,
MOSELEY.

You are requested to join your Battalion at Headquarters, at 9 o'clock _am Thursday 2__ inst.

(Signed) _Clifton 6 Levy_

Reproduced courtesy of the Royal Warwickshire Regimental Museum.

one week, far exceeding the target of 1,000. Thus three Birmingham City Battalions were formed, of which the third was designated the 16th Battalion of the Royal Warwickshire Regiment. Its commanding officer was Colonel D. F. Lewis, C.B., of Salford Priors, 'a retired officer who had gained distinction under Kitchener in the Soudan'.

New recruits to the 3rd Birmingham City Battalion
(Royal Warwickshire Regiment) lined up in front of 'Moseley College'.

The first two Battalions had 'two admirable sites ... placed at their disposal' by the Corporation of Sutton Coldfield and the men 'were fortunate in having such healthy quarters, with excellent facilities for bathing, boating, football and other recreations' as well as terrain suitable for 'physical and military drill' and combat practice. The third battalion 'was quartered less satisfactorily at Springfield College (Spring Hill College), Moseley'; 'the old theatre of the College had been converted into a dining hall, and washing accommodation had been provided in what was once the greenhouse'. The first task of the new recruits was to clean up the building, as reported in the Birmingham Daily Mail:

> *But one and all entered upon the necessary if somewhat irksome duties with splendid spirit. When a man who has handled nothing more substantial than a golf club, suddenly found himself armed with a cleaning mop; a bank clerk was detailed for the novel occupation of 'washing up' and sundry soft handed 'Birminghams' were told off to perform that duty detested of all dignified gardeners, clearing the drives of fallen leaves.*

The new recruits training at Spring Hill College during the First World War for service with the Royal Warwickshire Regiment.

Mobilisation of the battalion 'took longer than anticipated as it was soon realised the barracks could not accommodate a whole battalion comfortably'. After about 500 men had been called up, it became evident that there was insufficient sleeping accommodation for the rest; 'therefore billeting arrangements were hastily made with local Moseley residents'. An empty residence opposite the College, known as 'Windermere', was rented as Officers' Quarters.

Officers of the 3rd Birmingham Battalion on the steps of the principal's house. They were billeted across the road in the house known as 'Windermere'. Their commanding officer, Colonel Lewis, lived rather more comfortably at the Plough and Harrow Hotel, Hagley Road.

The recruits trained at the college 'until these men were ready to go into camp at Malvern' and subsequently to camps in Yorkshire, where they 'had a foretaste of privations to come', through ration shortages, night marches and floods.

All three 'Birmingham Pals Battalions' left Codford St. Mary on 21 November 1915, under orders for France.

> *Trench warfare had now begun in earnest. The world would have to wait almost another four long years for a war of movement to return. Until then the Western Front would become seemingly one long artillery duel. The infantry crouched in their trenches or sought cover in their dugouts, whilst each side tried to blow each other off the face of the earth.*

The 16th immediately found themselves in the thick of the fighting and were 'in the front line during Christmas, when the trenches were heavily bombarded'. Over the following year, the Battalion played a key role in the Somme offensive, in which 32 officers and 937 other ranks were killed and a number received military medals for gallantry and devotion to duty.

After September 1917, the Battalion entrained for the Ypres area and was ordered to dig a new line. The conditions were unspeakable:

> *In spite of heavy enemy shell fire and exceptional difficulties, the battalion finally reached its allotted position about 5 a.m. The weather conditions and mud were beyond description, and cases of men being swallowed up in shell craters and never being seen again were by no means uncommon.*
>
> *After holding the line for six days under most frightful shell fire in trenches knee-deep in mud and water, the battalion was ordered to attack Polderhoek Chateau at dawn on 9th October. The men were in a most deplorable condition and very weak, but in spite of this made a most magnificent effort to take the Chateau...*

Their heroic effort failed, as others had done before and were to do again – the Chateau remained in enemy hands until the last weeks of the war – and in those few days no fewer than 16 officers and 401 other ranks were killed or wounded. The Battalion 'was congratulated by the Brigade and Divisional Commanders on its great gallantry under appalling conditions'. Relieved of this nightmare, the Battalion then headed for Italy to train in the mountains near Padua. In stark contrast to previous years, Christmas Day 1917 'will long be remembered by all who lived to celebrate it. No fewer than 80 geese and 20 turkeys were served, and beef, oranges, nuts, cigarettes and beer were provided for the troops.'. This respite was followed by a long march to take over the line on the Piave from the Italians – 'the battalion again proved itself the best marching battalion in the Division, only dropping four men out of 700 in this march' – and a relatively uneventful few months until they were sent back to France in April 1918.

After a further gruelling stint 'holding the front line' and 'digging and wiring trenches' at St. Venant, after which the Brigadier 'specially congratulated all ranks on their splendid work, which, he said, stood out above that of the rest of the Brigade', the 16th played a distinguished role in the final British offensive. At Achiet le Petit, on the railway between Amiens and Arras, the Battalion under the command of a Birmingham officer, Lieutenant-Colonel Grahame Deakin, showed huge courage and initiative by storming and taking a railway embankment with 23 enemy machine guns on a 50-yards' front. The Divisional Commander described the whole attack as 'a very gallant piece of work' and added that 'the advance of the 16th Royal Warwickshire Regiment, without a check, to their final objective ... was especially brilliant'.

These 'city clerks' and other young professional workers who eagerly volunteered and found themselves learning to be soldiers at Spring Hill College could have had no idea of the horrors that they would encounter when they left the leafy confines of Moseley. They probably too had little sense of how heroically they would conduct themselves and of the plaudits and honours that would be heaped upon them. It therefore seems sad that 'owing to demobilisation being carried out individually and not in battalions, Birmingham had no opportunity of welcoming back those who were left of its gallant sons who formed the "Pals Brigade"'.

Back at 'Moseley Military Barracks', as the College was called during the war years, the intention was to maintain the building as an officers' training college but, owing to the government's economy campaign at the end of World War I, the scheme was dropped. Informal reports record that the building was briefly occupied by the Sisters of Nazareth who used it as an orphanage. However, the Congregation now at Nazareth House in London could find no reference in its archives, although the Sisters were based at the time of the First World War in Birmingham. Kelly's Directory shows Nazareth House to be located in Longbridge, Northfield in 1914-15, and in Rednal the following year, when it was described as a 'home for destitute, orphan and rescue children, also aged men and women'. The Directory for 1918 shows the first house in College Road to be 'Nazareth House, Sisters of Nazareth Orphan Home', in exactly the location which had been listed in 1915-17 as Moseley Military Barracks and in 1914 as the residence of 'Ross William (Spring Hill College)'. Therefore, we are unable to confirm that the Sisters of Nazareth were based temporarily at Moseley, although there is some evidence for it.

In 1921 the building came under the auspices of the Ministry of Labour. For two years, under the name Springfield College, it functioned as a teachers' training college for partially disabled ex-Servicemen, providing a slightly shortened course for some 150 men. They were selected from more than 1,000 applicants after a searching series of tests and interviews by a panel representing the Ministry of Pensions, the Board of Education and the National Union of Teachers. Despite its short life, the College was superbly run, and had its own magazine 'The Pathfinder'. One observer recalls:

> *The experiment was an inspired one, boldly conceived and thoroughly executed, and it was amply justified by the results. The Principal, the Vice-Principal and the tutors were all ex-Servicemen, and they constituted a brilliant staff, much admired and respected by every man in the college. So excellent was their work that Springfield College men became known far and wide for their cultural background and their ability as teachers.*

1921-22. The building, then known as Springfield College, being used as an emergency Teacher Training College for partially disabled ex-servicemen.

The Principal Colonel Morris was acclaimed as a man of 'kindliness and uprightness, whose inspiration came from the highest ideals and whose labours erected a monument more lasting than brass'. The extent of his legacy can be judged by the fact that a reunion of former students in 1938 revealed that more than 80 per cent had become head teachers.

But this was intended only as an emergency post-war measure and in 1923 the County Borough Council of Birmingham took over the building for conversion to a school. At 10 a.m. on 11 September 1923, the Moseley Secondary School opened. The conversion to a school is described in Chapter 4, but first we trace the origins of Moseley School from the founding of the College Road Board School in 1900.

References and acknowledgements

This chapter draws on the following sources: The Moseleian, particularly 'The School 1857-1948' by B. Hargrove (July 1948); Birmingham newspapers of the time; a letter by Edgar C. Sheppard entitled 'Moseley Village' in a newspaper cutting which is undated; Pine Dell concert programmes (1893-1898); the Moseley Society Journal, various editions; Kelly's Directories; R.H. Brazier and E. Sandford, Birmingham and the Great War 1914-1919 (1921); T. Carter, Birmingham Pals (1997); and various contemporary and historical accounts held in the Local Studies section of the Birmingham Central Library. Our thanks to Pete Anstey for the photograph of the bath houses; the Sisters of Nazareth, Nazareth House, London; and Vanessa Harbar, Assistant Curator of the Royal Regiment of Fusiliers Museum (Royal Warwickshire), Warwick, which holds documents and photographs of the 3rd Birmingham Battalion.

Chapter Three

College Road Board School 1900-1955

The story of Moseley School really began in 1900 when the Yardley School Board founded the College Road Board School. Much of South Birmingham remained in the Parish of Yardley in the County of Worcestershire until it was incorporated into Birmingham in 1911. Under the 1870 Education Act, local ratepayers elected School Boards with powers to build and maintain Board Schools at the ratepayers' expense. Remarkably for the times, women were entitled to stand for election to School Boards, a right which was taken away when the School Board system was abolished by the 1902 Act.

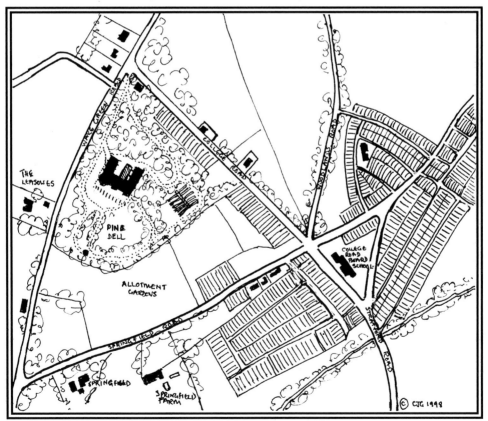

By the early 1900s housing development had swallowed up most of the farmland, leaving just the main building of Grove Farm still standing. College Road Board School was built to serve this expanding population. The Pine Dell Hydropathic Establishment, meanwhile, had closed its doors to visitors but was still listed as the residence of Mr William Ross.

Board Schools opened up educational opportunity to a whole section of society which had previously been denied it. Birmingham, led by its radical MP George Dixon, had fought hard for this reform and immediately began building Board Schools. The Parish of Yardley, which was less densely populated, followed more slowly. College Road was one of its first Board Schools. Built on land between College Road, Springfield Road and Stratford Road, it housed Infants, Girls and Boys Departments, each with its own Head and staff. The original building, now much extended, must have been an imposing sight when its elaborate facade dominated the surrounding area.

1900. Yardley College Road Board School.

Each department began with about 100 children but numbers rose rapidly and by 1903 each had between 400-450. The Inspectors' report considered 'many classes much too large for effective teaching'. It was a constantly changing school population, however, with large numbers leaving each term as they reached the School Leaving Age (originally 12, then 13 and after 1918, 14) and others being admitted.

City of Birmingham Education Committee

SCHOLAR'S LEAVING CERTIFICATE

This is to Certify that . . .

has attended the..School

for ....years,...........months, and is legally exempt from attendance at an Elementary School, having either passed an Examination by H.M. Inspector of Schools, in Reading, Writing, and Arithmetic in the 7th Standard or reached the age of 14 years, as defined by Section 9 of the Education Act, 1918.

Standard completed..

Percentage of Attendance..

Punctuality..

Conduct..

General Remarks..

....

....

Head Teacher.

Date............................ 192

Chief Education Officer.

A Leaving Certificate from the 1920s.

Within the first few years, control of the school had passed to Worcestershire County Council as the 1902 Act abolished School Boards. By 1904 Yardley Secondary (later Grammar) School had been opened and, as other secondary and commercial schools followed, College Road lost more and more of its successful older pupils each year, provided their parents could pay the fees. By the 1920s so many pupils were passing on to secondary schools that the Inspectors' report concluded that 'it would be unreasonable to expect a much higher standard of work' in the older classes. More girls than boys passed the examination for secondary schools but far fewer girls were able to take up their places. In 1913, for example, 23 girls passed but only five could afford to go.

Attendance seemed to be the main preoccupation in the early days. The Clerk to the School Board visited every two weeks to check the registers and the attendance rate was recorded every week in the school's Log Book, together with the reasons for poor attendance. These reasons varied from 'lack of coal to heat the boiler' and 'heavy falls of snow' to epidemics of measles, scarlet fever and diphtheria which occurred several times a year and sometimes resulted in the school being closed for several weeks. The spread of such infections must have been encouraged by class sizes of up to 75 and by poor ventilation. Inspectors' reports refer constantly to 'defective ventilation' and the lack of 'efficient extract for foul air'. In 1910 the Medical Officer of Health ruled that 'the school should be closed and thoroughly cleaned'.

The Board of Education Inspectors who visited the school every year were, however, more impressed with the quality of education. After only one year they judged that 'teaching is sound and the school promises to take a high position' but they too were concerned about attendance. In 1907 they reported that 'instruction is of good quality and discipline excellent but attendance is very irregular'. The school tried to encourage the children by awarding '10 minutes extra play' on Friday afternoons for the best attenders and by punishing truancy more severely than almost any other misdemeanour. Four or six strokes of the cane were usual for truants whereas 'shooting with elastic' and 'using indecent language' only merited two.

Mrs Alice Rose (nee Barker), who was a pupil at a nearby Board School in the early years of the century, has described a typical school day. The girls arrived at 9.00 and assembled for prayers and a hymn. The morning was spent on reading, writing and arithmetic or 'going to a large house lent to the school for housewifery, cookery or laundry'. In the afternoons there was sewing, knitting, darning or painting and, on certain days, history or geography. Playtime was fifteen minutes in the middle of the morning and afternoon. Dinnertime lasted two hours as all children walked home, sometimes quite long distances. Alice remembers, at the age of four and a half, being responsible for taking her two and a half year old brother to and from school. She herself had started school at the same age in 1906.

A Board School class in 1912. Alice Barker, as she then was, is third from the right in the third row. The stiff white collars worn by many of the boys indicate that they came from a charitable 'home'.

There were no specialist facilities in the early days and the school concentrated on a fairly basic curriculum – reading, writing, arithmetic, dictation, grammar, recitation and drill. Alice describes drill as 'bending and doing exercises with the arms'. Drawing, singing and science were soon introduced at College Road as well as cookery, sewing, knitting and laundry for the girls. Classes were regularly tested by the Headteacher and children were promoted and demoted. Adjustments were also made to the timetable to reflect progress. In the school's first year the Head of the Girls' Department reported that 'arithmetic is very weak. Extra time will be devoted to it'. Back to basics in 1901! In 1913 the Inspectors' report required that 'children should speak with more distinct enunciation'. Circumstances could also dictate timetable changes as in July 1901 when 'writing lessons replaced oral lessons on account of the great heat'.

Despite the utilitarian nature of much of the timetable, the school did its best to provide an interesting environment for the children. In 1902 when the school had only just 'been supplied with a bell which, I think, will be of great assistance in forming habits of punctuality', twelve framed pictures were delivered to be hung in the classrooms and the hall. Later five statues were placed in the hall! There were displays in museum cases and concerts were given to raise money to buy library books for each classroom. A 'tennis club was formed for the Upper Classes of the Girls' Department' as early as 1903. Improvements to the building were a mixed blessing, however, as in 1905 'hammering this week has greatly interfered with the lessons'. It was possible to take classes 'out into the lanes and fields to gather specimens for their nature-work'. Not all pupils responded to this cultured atmosphere; boys were frequently punished for 'following girls into the Girls' lavatories' and on one occasion 10 boys were 'thrashed on the buttocks for interfering with girls' clothing in class'!

All three departments began with very young teachers. Mr George Henry Edwards, Headteacher of the Boys' Department was 31 and the rest of the staff were in their early twenties. All had been trained for one year, at the Teacher Training College at Saltley. They were required to 'keep a weekly record of work in an exercise book, which is to comprise all the work which the teacher thinks he can manage during the week'. Mr Edwards remained at the school for 33 years and the first Head of the Girls' Department, Miss Mary Agnes Sewards, for 25 years. But the staff around them were constantly changing. When a vacancy occurred, the Headteachers would visit local schools looking for a suitable replacement.

St. Peter's College Saltley, built as an Anglican Training College in the 1850s, trained many of the Board School teachers.

There were many different categories of teacher including pupil-teachers who had only just left school themselves. Uncertificated teachers were often absent to take their examinations and all teachers could be sent to another school in the city at short notice; by 1911 Birmingham had taken over the running of the school from Worcestershire. In the 1920s extra teachers were appointed 'for the very backward children'. Perhaps they had found out that class size does matter! Male and female teachers used the cane to deal with 'talking', 'disobedience', 'disorder in line' and even 'laughing'. Caning was usually on the hand and boys were caned far more often than girls. Alice Rose remembers that it was 'rare that children were fetched out in front of the class' but the same names appear in the Punishment Book, casting some doubt on its deterrent effect.

Like the pupils, teachers frequently suffered from infectious illnesses and any hospital treatment usually meant an absence of many weeks. But not all absences were for unfortunate reasons. In March 1906 one teacher 'received a telegram ... to play in a league football match' and the Head of the Girls' Department was given leave of absence for 'a most delightful trip to the Italian Lakes'. At first only men taught in the Boys' Department and only women in the Girls' and Infants'. Staff shortages soon meant that it was necessary to move teachers around to fill the gaps. This was particularly true during the war years when few men remained, although the rule preventing married women from continuing to teach stayed in place until 1939.

The First World War affected the school in many ways. The children were sent home on several occasions 'as we had no coal to heat the boiler'. They knitted socks for the soldiers and collected candles to be sent to the trenches. They collected fruit for wounded soldiers and in January 1916 sent 18 parcels of food to the front. Several teachers left to join up and others were given leave 'to see a friend off to the front' or because of 'special war circumstances'. The school acquired an allotment and began growing vegetables. When the war ended, there was barely time to celebrate the Armistice before schools closed owing to the epidemic of Spanish Influenza which lasted for three months.

Despite their efforts to help the soldiers, many of the children needed charitable help themselves. In the coldest winters, the teachers made soup for the poorest children using vegetables sent by friends. Tickets for bread were issued. In 1904 the Headteacher referred to 'some very sad cases of children being underfed and badly clothed' and in 1909 free breakfasts were introduced. Many consignments of boots were sent to the school 'for needy children' and the Relief Committee supplied books. Children whose parents lost their jobs or their homes had to be placed in charitable institutions. Alice Rose remembers that of the 46 children in her age group, 16 were boys from a 'home' who wore a distinctive uniform and were marched to and from school. The building shown as 'Springfield' on maps of the area was a similar home for girls, most of whom attended College Road School. There were frequent

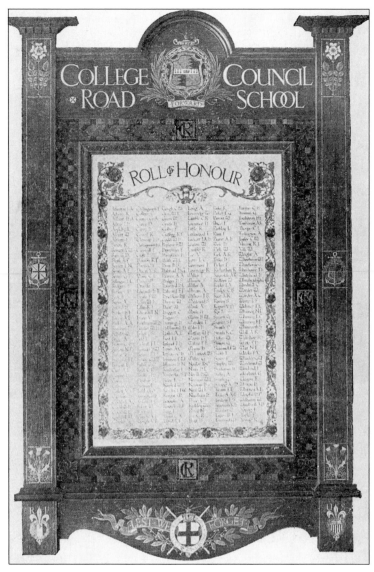

Many of College Road's former pupils, having started school around 1900, were just the right age to volunteer in 1914. Many, as the Roll of Honour shows, did not come back.

exclusions from school for cases of TB and scabies as the 1918 Education Act introduced medical inspections.

Many schools in Birmingham served much poorer areas than College Road, however, and throughout the 1920s and 1930s the school was involved in charitable work. A deprived inner-city school was 'adopted' and parents (in what was then an area of high employment and relative prosperity) donated parcels of clothing to be sent. The children gave up their traditional Christmas party and provided a party and presents for 50 poor children. Each year they collected 'enormous quantities of fruit and vegetables to be sent' and parents lent their cars to transport the produce. They also raised money for causes such as 'orphans of the Titanic', the fund to build a Shakespeare Memorial Theatre and the Children's Hospital.

Life for schoolchildren was not all hardship and deprivation. Birmingham did its best to enrich the educational experience provided by its Board Schools. Violin classes were available as early as 1911 at College Road and the children made visits to art exhibitions and concerts. A gramophone was provided from School Fund for music appreciation, libraries were purchased by subscription and the school won trophies in the Midland Music Festival. In the early years there was an annual outing to Sutton Park and a day off for 'The Hall Green Races'. Later, older pupils were taken to London and Stratford.

A class at College Road Board School, with their teacher, in the early years of the century. Efforts have obviously been made to brighten up the classroom.

Despite 'problems with the smallness of the field and the rather large number of schools using it', the school was building a strong reputation for sporting success winning trophies in a number of different team competitions. In 1925, following the appointment of Miss Minnie Woodhouse as Head of the Girls' Department, new school colours – emerald and scarlet – were introduced and 'school caps with badges were sold to the children'. Prefects were appointed and a house system was set up – using the names of Oxford and Cambridge colleges!

In 1927, in response to the demand for extended schooling, a major building programme was begun to provide specialist rooms. This necessitated a temporary increase in class sizes and the removal of several classes to the Primitive Methodist

Church in Springfield Road. This work prepared the way for the reorganisation of the school into Infants, Junior Mixed and Senior Mixed Departments in 1934; Mr Shakespeare took charge of the Juniors and Miss Mason of the Seniors. In the same year 108 copies of the first school magazine were sold priced at 3d. The Inspectors considered that 'this School is fortunate in its children, the majority of whom not only enjoy good home conditions but also have a wider range of experiences than children less favourably placed'.

The schools did not have many years of calm before the next upheaval. The Second World War had a far greater impact than the First. On 31 August 1939 the school closed at 4.30 for children to be evacuated and it reopened in October on a voluntary basis. By the following August it was considered safe to open in Compulsory Session again but lessons were frequently interrupted by Air Raid alerts throughout that autumn. On 18 October the roof was damaged 'by masonry hurled from explosions in Solihull Road and Knowle Road'. The day often started late following 'severe air raid of previous night'. In November buses took the children to the station for evacuation to Loughborough. Some remained at College Road and the teachers shuttled backwards and forwards until all returned in May 1941. In 1942 the school opened as a Rest Centre serving up to 200 breakfasts and was also used for the reception of evacuees from the London area.

Throughout all this, the life of the school continued with remarkable normality; the choir sang all over the city, plays were performed and PE demonstrations were given. In 1944 the school collected £956 for 'Salute the Soldiers' week. The aftermath of war can be seen in the inauguration of free milk for children and the arrival of 48 parcels of food from Australia. Cigarettes must have been more readily available as smoking now became the most common offence to merit the cane!

The school gradually returned to normal, still with classes being taught in an annexe at Springfield Road Methodist Chapel as numbers continued to grow. But more changes lay ahead. The Butler Education Act of 1944 had paved the way for the allocation of children at the age of 11 to Grammar, Technical or Modern Schools according to their supposed aptitudes. In 1951 Mr Isaac became Head of the Junior School and the following year Miss Cohen was appointed Head of the Senior School. It was therefore her job to explain to parents the introduction of the new Entrance Examination – the 11-plus. In 1953 a total of 111 candidates sat Part 1 of the Entrance Examination, 46 did well enough to sit Part 2 and 33 finally passed.

Miss Cohen had been appointed to implement the transition from College Road Senior School to the new Moseley Modern Mixed School. Birmingham had decided to provide three of the new modern schools with purpose-built accommodation. Moseley Modern was built on the site just across College Road formerly used as playing fields by King Edward's Camp Hill. On 20 July 1955 the Senior School closed in the afternoon 'a day earlier because of packing of books for transfer' and the next morning the staff and 40 children assembled in school ready for moving. A former pupil recalls 'we had to carry books and equipment up the road'. The building now became the home of Springfield Junior and Infants School and Moseley Modern Mixed School was born.

The building, with many additions, is now home to Springfield Junior and Infants School.

References and acknowledgements

Information in this chapter comes mainly from the complete collection of Log Books and Punishment Books kindly made available by Liz Rose, Headteacher of Springfield Junior and Infants School, and from documents held by Moseley School and the Local Studies section of the Birmingham Central Library. Our thanks to Richard Trengrouse for the loan of family photographs and to Jack Barker and Alice Rose (nee Barker) for their first-hand accounts.

Chapter Four

Moseley Secondary (later Grammar) School 1923-1955

1923 was an unusual year for a new secondary school to open. It was the year when a formidable package of government cuts, which become known as 'the Geddes axe' after the businessman who chaired the committee, was due to take effect in an attempt to reduce the massive public debt and recover the economy after the First World War. Education was one of the prime targets, with class sizes set to increase to 50, teachers' salaries to be reduced, the school starting age raised to six, secondary school fees increased and free places for scholarship children restricted.

The proposals provoked strong protests from many quarters, including teachers' organisations, trade unions and the Labour Party. Their dismay at the damage likely to be inflicted on education was all the more acute because the mood of the times had seen a developing faith in educational expansion as the way forward. Some of the reasons for this went back to the important Education Act of 1902, which replaced the School Boards with Local Education Authorities and introduced state aid for secondary schools. For the first time, Britain had the makings of a proper system of secondary education.

But the way in which the Conservative government of the time chose to shape the system, made it elitist and selective on the basis of social class and ability to pay rather than intellectual capability. There were not to be too many secondary or 'grammar' schools and they must charge fees and adopt many of the characteristics of the great public schools: a curriculum which included Latin and Greek and less science and vocational subjects; no examinations either on entry or departure; teachers who were untrained but from public school and Oxbridge backgrounds; school uniforms, crests and mottoes (preferable in Latin); and playing fields to allow for organised team games, notably rugby and cricket. The central authorities looked favourably on schools with an ancient foundation or endowment (like the King Edward VI schools in Birmingham), while pressurising those which the School Boards had developed for their older, cleverer elementary school children (like George Dixon, Waverley and Central Schools) into imitating the 'grammar school' model.

The main result was to exclude the vast majority of ordinary children from continuing their education, and they consequently spent their whole school lives in elementary schools until they could leave at 14. The one concession – the introduction in 1907 of a proportion of free places in grammar schools – helped some children, but also introduced into elementary schools an early form of selection, with all the cramming, disappointment and wastage later associated with the 11-plus examination.

A number of Local Education Authorities, especially the larger urban ones like Birmingham, were acutely aware that the education system constituted by the 1902 Act was failing most of their children. Their hopes of wide-spread change had to be postponed during the war years, but 1918 saw a major Education Act which, full of expansionist plans and pointing towards secondary education for all, appeared to be a pledge for the future. By that time, the existing secondary schools were bursting at the seams, yet there was no room for thousands of children who had qualified for a place. Overall less than one in ten elementary school pupils were able to proceed to secondary school.

In 1920 Birmingham Education Committee provided elementary education for nearly 150,000 children, and was directly responsible for just eight 'council secondary schools' accommodating 2,500 pupils. It also made grants to 10 'aided secondary schools' (3,500 pupils), including the seven schools of the King Edward VI Foundation and two Roman Catholic schools. There were many more places for boys than girls, especially in the aided schools which were all single-sex institutions. In response to the 1918 Act, the Committee submitted a major scheme of expansion, involving a capital outlay of £400,000 and including plans for many new schools on housing estates and for more secondary school places.

National economic problems through much of the 1920s and 1930s, along with Birmingham's struggle to keep pace with its ever-growing elementary school population, were to hamper progress, and most plans had to be shelved. Even where sites had been acquired, the building work could not be funded, leading to a 'very modest' amount of growth. Moseley School for Boys was therefore fortunate to be one of the only two new secondary schools to come to fruition (the other was Saltley Mixed in 1928), and the decision to convert an existing building can be appreciated in the light of the prevailing financial constraints.

An early description of the Moseley Secondary School depicted it as 'a mere shell – a conglomeration of bricks and mortar, picturesque, but totally unsuitable as a school, and set in the midst of a veritable forest.' Certainly much of the 1920s was spent in renovating and converting the building, confirming the impression that the Education Committee – fortunately for later generations of Moseleians – bought it in rather a hurry and discovered its shortcomings afterwards.

For the reasons outlined above, the Committee was looking to expand its secondary school provision after the War and had acquired sites in South Birmingham for separate boys' and girls' schools. Then the possibility of the Moseley building cropped up, made available by the Government's Disposal

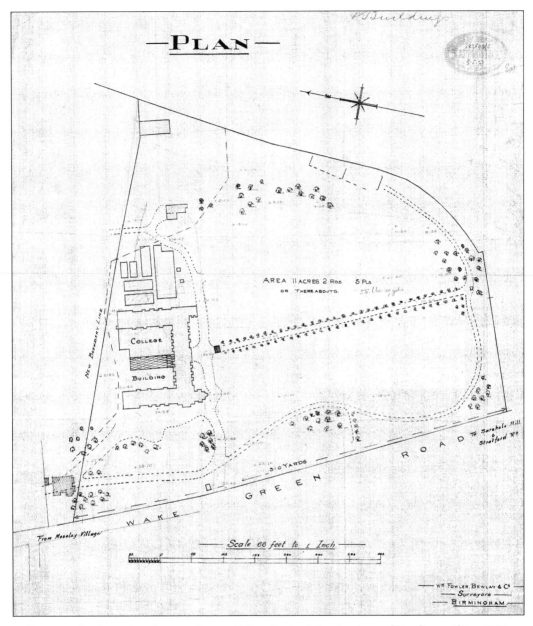

Surveyor's plans for the purchase of the site by Birmingham City Council in 1923.

and Liquidation Board because the Ministry of Labour no longer needed it for the training of ex-servicemen which had gone on there as Springfield College. The Birmingham Education Committee heard that it was an 'imposing structure' with a frontage of 310 yards, that a reduced price of £7,500 had been offered 'in order to assist your Council in a matter of public and local interest', and that its acquisition would enable them to open a secondary school at least a year earlier than if they built from scratch.

In March 1923, the purchase was agreed and approval sought from the Board of Education in London for recognition of Moseley Council Secondary School, a school for 400 boys, from September 1923. Plans for an equivalent school for 400 girls at Queensbridge were subsequently deferred, confirming the Committee's wisdom in pressing ahead with Moseley when the opportunity arose.

However, the Committee was embarking on seven years of heavy spending which they had not fully anticipated. The school was expected to function initially in 'certain rooms in the front of the building' and the temporary huts and laboratories erected for Springfield College. An early warning, in May 1923, came from the Architect, who reported that 'the condition of some parts of the building is very poor … it is not possible to get tenders for this work', but plans proceeded in a thoroughly optimistic way. It was not difficult to recruit the first 100 boys, because the city's Secondary Schools Examination always produced more successful candidates than there were places for; indeed the Council had heard in January 1923 that even 'free place' pupils could not be accommodated. On the Board of Education's insistence, parents of other intending pupils had been warned that fees were likely to rise from the £4 per annum charged in Birmingham's municipal secondary schools to 'at least £9'.

Mr E.H. Robinson,
Headmaster 1923-1955

The recruitment of Moseley's teaching staff was initiated by the appointment of Ernest H. Robinson as Headmaster, from a field of 214 applicants. Mr – or Major – Robinson had gained a modern languages degree and a teaching qualification at Cambridge University and, at 33, had taught for just six years in a Nottinghamshire grammar school. This period had been interrupted by four and a half years' distinguished war service in the Shropshire Light Infantry, for which he had been awarded the Distinguished Service Order and the Military Cross. Moseley folklore later had it that the appointing committee, impressed that 'the little blighter practically held up the German Army on his own', chose him because 'if he could command soldiers in battle, four or five hundred boys should not be beyond him'. His starting salary was £650.

Four assistant masters (Messrs Hughes, Andrews, Brampton and Midgley) were appointed to open the school with Mr Robinson, with three more appointments (Messrs Jones, Hill and Gillespie) in the pipeline. Nearly all of them, like the Head, were relatively young and inexperienced, but well qualified in their subjects and trained as teachers, which was quite unusual for secondary schoolteachers at the time. Some had had to interrupt their education to serve in the war; Cyril Midgley, for example, joined up as an 18 year old and was so badly gassed that he suffered attacks while teaching and had to retire in 1931.

The original staff appointed in 1923.
Back row left to right: Messrs Gillespie, Hill, Brampton, Jones
Front row left to right: Messrs Hughes, Robinson, Midgley, Andrews.

The Burnham salary scale having recently been introduced, they were paid between about £250 and £320 per annum, rising by annual £15 increments, to either £500 or £550, though it is not clear why some got more than others. These original eight staff together were to complete an amazing 230 years' service at Moseley and therefore played a major part in shaping the new school. Some of the other staff appointed to the school in the early years also became long-serving stalwarts, such as Messrs Lambert, Bush, Waugh, Smith and Constable, but the record for long service is held by Mr Line, who spent his entire career (1926-1970) teaching mathematics at Moseley.

Mr Robinson was appointed in July 1923; Moseley Secondary School opened on 11 September. Not surprisingly, it was far from ready and on the first morning, 'hardly any preparations had been made. Most of the rooms were bare and thick with dust, and those in the tower were in an unbelievable state, having been used by generations of pigeons and crows as nesting places.' One of the original masters recalled 'our first staff meeting in a room with an empty packing-case for our only furniture, and an inch and a half of black fluffy dust on the floor. On that first day there were no pens, paper, ink and books on the desks for the pupils.' A handbell summoned 99 boys in from the school field – or rather from the trees which they had been climbing – and they were greeted in the library before being sent home for three weeks while the staff did their best to get part of the building ready.

Within a week, the first of many alarm bells was rung by the Architect, who reported that 'the building is in very poor condition, and a large number of repairs are having to be undertaken. Quite half of the floor to the large assembly hall has had to be replaced owing to the presence of dry rot. Dry rot has been found in many other floors and extensive repairs are having to be made to the roofs, chimneys and gutters'. A month later, he said that 'the dilapidated condition on the building is becoming more and more apparent as work proceeds', and then 'since my last report it has been found necessary to take down several large chimneys which were in a dangerous condition' and in the gymnasium (now the hall) 'a close watch must be kept on the woodwork in the future, though the [glass] roof is perfectly safe'. In February 1924, in uncanny anticipation of architects' reports of the 1990s, he drew attention to the dry rot in the library which was 'endangering the safety of this roof. I consider it essential that tie rods should be put in to guard against a further spread of this roof which has already thrust the front wall out of line several inches'.

Birmingham Education Committee agreed to spend £10,000 on converting the building, plus £3,705 for furniture, over a four year period. The most urgent need was for an effective heating system, which was duly – and noisily – installed during the first term, to be followed a year later by replacement of the 'historic and leaky gas illumination' by 'handsome' electric lighting as the school took advantage of the electric cables being laid past the entrance and down Wake Green Road. The first phase of building work included substantial alteration to the west wing to accommodate classrooms, and in the Autumn

PROPOSED SECONDARY SCHOOL AT MOSELEY.

It will be recalled that the proposal to open a new Secondary School for Boys at Spring Hill College, Moseley, involves an expenditure of approximately £10,000 in alterations and repairs, plus £3,705 for furniture, such expenditure being spread over a period of four years. In order that the building may be ready for occupation in September, it is necessary that the work should be commenced as soon as possible, and your Sub-Committee accordingly recommend that, subject to the approval of the City Council, the Board of Education and the Ministry of Health, the following tenders be accepted, and that the Town Clerk be instructed to prepare contracts, where necessary, with authority to affix the Corporate Common Seal thereto :—

Work.	Contractor.	£	s.	d.
New heating apparatus ...	Messrs. Brightside Foundry and Engineering Co., Ltd. ...	525	0	0
Structural alterations ...	Mr. L. Gorton	365	0	0
Gas and plumbing work...	,, E. J. Sands ...	183	9	1
Colouring and painting ...	., B. Gay	415	0	0
		£1,488	9	1

In addition to the above, it is estimated that the cost of repairs for which it is not possible to obtain tenders will be £861 10s. 11d., while the cost of the furniture is estimated at £1,125. It is now recommended that the City Council be asked to authorise the borrowing of the total sum of £3,775, the amount required to complete the first portion of the scheme.

Extract from the minutes of the Schools Sub-Committee to the City Council; these proved to be rather optimistic figures.

Term of 1925, the Fourth Forms moved into the first floor and the Third Forms to the ground floor. A whole new upper corridor was grafted onto the existing brickwork at the rear of the main building to link the west and east wings.

At Mr Robinson's request, some improvements were made to the ventilation, light and soundproofing of classrooms and to the quantity of 'lavatory basins for washing after games', as well as enhancements (a kitchen, bathroom and lavatory) to the Headmaster's house because 'Mr Robinson does not care to occupy in its present condition'. The rent for the house was then fixed at £60 plus rates, with residency a requirement of the job, and the Robinsons – newly married in December 1923 – moved in to the house. As their successors, the Gaskin family, were later to find, this 'living on the job' – especially with the house overlooking the playing fields – enabled a closeness of involvement with school affairs familiar to boarding school life but a rarity in the maintained sector of education.

The Education Committee was soon seeing grander prospects for the new school, with a revised building plan raising its accommodation to 500 in due course, at an estimated cost of £20,500. There would be six classrooms each for 25 boys, six for 30 and four for 35, and, replacing the inherited huts, new

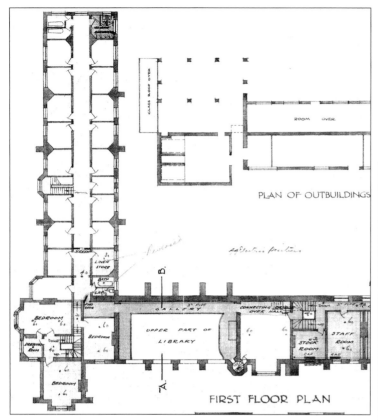

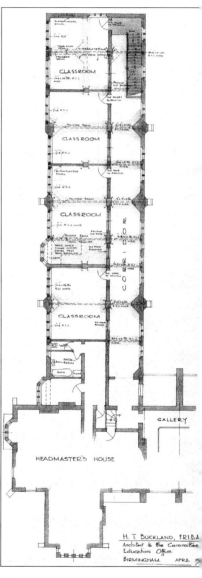

Architects' plan of the west wing before alteration in 1925, showing the students' study bedrooms and the gallery leading to the connecting bridge over the entrance hall.

The central corridor of the west wing has been altered and the 15 bedrooms converted into 4 class-rooms.

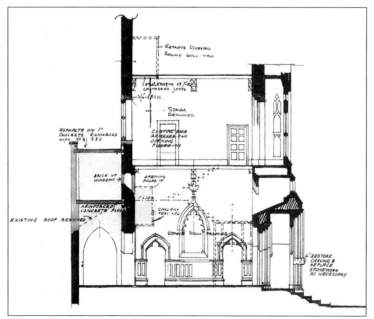

This section through the entrance hall facing the war memorial shows how the sloping roof of the 'cloister' style corridor was removed in 1925 and a first floor corridor added, as the previous access via the gallery and connecting bridge was unsuitable for a school.

chemistry and physics laboratories, a manual instruction room and dining facilities, as well as sheds for 200 bicycles, reflecting the most popular mode of schoolboy transport at the time. The editor of the school magazine, The Moseleian, seemed to be finding the seemingly endless building work too much in early 1926 when he wrote of

> *... the great inconvenience to practically everyone. One form is home-less; the members of others make their way to their rooms in fear and trembling; the air in the Masters' Common Room is thick with brick dust; and even the Head Master has been driven from his sanctum. The sounds with which we are most familiar in these days are the clink of hammer, trowel and pick, the rumble of falling bricks, the gargle of the Ford, and the hiss of the steam lorry.*

At this time the sign outside the school read MOSELEY SECONDARY SCHOOL – BRICKLAYERS REQUIRED. No wonder that the General Strike of May 1926 was welcomed for bringing 'an almost idyllic calm to our tortured precincts', though it encouraged a few boys to stay at home while others 'performed prodigies of pedestrianism'.

When work resumed, the new entrance hall and staircase were completed, linking the lower corridor to the new upper one and giving access to the Masters' Common Room in the tower. The editor of The Moseleian praised the workmen for their energy and skill and observed that 'the thought of the wonderful school which they are building for us fills some of us with a sort of awed pleasure'. By Easter 1927, 'great joy' was expressed at the opening of the excellent new Gymnasium in the east wing, with cloakrooms and a dining hall to be located in the 'cavernous depths' beneath. These 'depths' were part of the original nineteenth century cloisters or 'undercroft' which, because of the lie of the land, were deeper on the east side. 'Spacious and lofty', the new Gymnasium would permit 'future Moseleians to be trained to hold their own against all comers in matters of sport and physical fitness'. It does seem to have been a particularly generously proportioned and well equipped example of its type – and is still largely unchanged today.

The new Science wing was the next main task. The Moseleian of Summer 1926 commented on 'the wanderings of the Science Staff' who, 'homeless for a time, have found a haven of rest for their beloved huts alongside the dismantled boiler house'. Uncharitable remarks from schoolboy contributors about 'the stinks' (the normal public school nickname for science laboratories) suggested that this location had its advantages. However, construction of the new wing – to the east of the old east wing – got under way, but was 'seriously delayed by the discovery of a disused well. Many weeks elapsed, and much additional expense was incurred, where the foundations were complete'. This surprise finding was to be repeated in the 1990s during the installation of a new fire escape when, it became clear that this was no ordinary well. The new block, comprising four classrooms, an Art room and Science laboratories, was completed and occupied during the Autumn Term of 1927 and with it, the introduction of a new system by which each master had a room and the boys moved around instead of vice versa.

The opening of the new Gymnasium had released the 'old' Gym, originally the sizeable swimming bath of the hydropathic establishment, for Handicraft lessons, but it was intended to have a more auspicious future as the school's new Assembly Hall. In May 1928 the leaky glass roof was dismantled and it was found necessary to demolish much of the brickwork and rebuild with 'massive-looking girders'; only the stage part of the hall survived. It was correctly observed during construction that 'judging by outward appearances, the new Hall will be a very fine one, quite in keeping with the noble architecture of the original School buildings', and it all took over a year.

By Easter of 1929, it was thought that the slow progress was due to problems with the interior decorations in the style of Modern Symbolic Art – and they are indeed remarkable. According to Moseley folklore, Mr Robinson felt that some of the rather well-developed nymphs were unsuitable for a boys' school and insisted on some flattening of the relief, producing the rather androgynous-looking figures which are still so impressive. Repainting in the 1970s also highlighted the sculptures with some amusing results, described in Chapter Six, and now, after re-decorating in 1998, their full elegance can be appreciated.

An example of the decorative bas-reliefs in the new Assembly Hall.
A strange choice indeed for a boys' school!

Some ten years after the building of the Hall, Mr Robinson was able to raise the funds to put the 'finishing touches' – oak panelling, with matching desk, chair and lectern. Rather more humdrum but probably as popular with the boys was the asphalting of the various 'quads' between wings as playgrounds, which more or less brought to a close the phase of intensive building which had occupied most of the 1920s and created Moseley School as it was to remain for half a century.

The grounds were also reshaped in the early days with the felling of trees to enlarge the playing field, though others round the edge were left to 'preserve the amenities of the property'. The imposing avenue down the middle of the field

The building in which Moseley Secondary School opened in 1923, shown here after the first phase of alterations to the grounds.

was removed during December 1923 under the post-war Unemployment Relief Works scheme, the Architect at one point reporting that the amount of 'big timber' lying about was 'obstructing further operations' for the builders. He did suggest, though, that the second access to the rear of the school made to facilitate the timber felling should become permanent, with the addition of a pair of oak gates and fencing. Improvements continued over many years, with extra small areas added to the playing fields as more trees were removed, levelling and rolling undertaken and, at Mr Robinson's request, a groundsman appointed in 1926. An early pupil recalled that impositions (punishments) were often to remove 100 weeds or stones from the field and the first 'sports day' was rumoured to include an obstacle race over the tree stumps.

Other improvements to the grounds included the laying out of a lawn in front of the west wing and of garden beds along the Wake Green frontage, in anticipation of the much-needed widening of the road. The mature trees which still border the road by the school are no doubt a legacy of this scheme, though it was 1934 before a safe footpath was created and boys relieved of having to cross 'a road upon which traffic has multiplied so greatly in the past few years'. A nice addition was the planting of bulbs amongst the trees by the road, and the following year, the provision of street lighting – grotesquely purple, thought one pupil – dispelled 'the ancestral dimness' of the road forever.

There were some regrets about these 'improvements' as, for example, when The Moseleian's editor wrote of 'mixed feelings' in January 1928 on viewing 'the scene of desolation':

> *That noble and picturesque belt of trees was admired by all, and seemed a part of the individuality of the school, and we cannot but mourn their passing. Some of them were land-marks; a certain holly-bush, for instance, had associations for many. The disappearance of these old friends, however, is not without its compensations. The regularity with which boys injured themselves by falling from trees had become quite monotonous.*

A significant day was 23 July 1928 when 'a familiar School landmark', the Obelisk inscribed *'Dux femina facti'*, was removed from its place at the end of the field. The school magazine recounted how, on the occasion of the School versus Masters Cricket match:

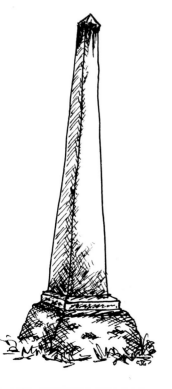

> *The removal of this historic piece of stone was effected by means of a very small trolley and a large display of ingenuity by a resourceful foreman, who got together a 'scratch' team of hauliers consisting of the Head Master and members of the batting side (the boys). These he encouraged with cheerful shouts of 'Gee! My lads!' occasionally allowing them to 'have a blow' and finally the obelisk was dragged to the School gates. Further engineering difficulties arising, it was not until 9 p.m. that the old monument started on its reluctant journey to Oxford, where, we understand, it is now to be found in the grounds of Mansfield College.*

The obelisk honouring the College's founders was removed to Mansfield College in the late 1920s, sustaining some damage during the move.

At Moseley, the vacated space was soon occupied by a 'small and unpretentious pavilion' (or wooden shack, as it appeared in the 1950s) in time for the cricket season.

As to what went on inside the school building, the original intake of 99 boys was divided into four forms, labelled 2A, 2B, 2C and 2D, and by Christmas 1923 into four houses – Mansfield, Glover, James and Springfield. The first three derived their names from the founders of Spring Hill College, the last from the school's immediate institutional predecessor. Nicknamed 'Spring', it was renamed Midgley in tribute to its first housemaster on the occasion of his premature retirement from teaching.

The importance attached to the house system and the prefects who presided over it was one of the ways in which Moseley assumed the trappings of traditional public/grammar school life. Others included the daily morning assembly accompanied by the Library organ, and the adoption of school colours – initially and temporarily black and white, with red soon added, in line with a number of other organisations in the Moseley area – and of a school crest or 'Arms of the School'. This was based on those of the philanthropist John Howard which appeared in the old building, and the heraldic description reads: 'Gules a bend argent between six crosses crosslet fitchee or, the whole within a bordure ermine'; the crosses crosslet fitchee were swords.

Later, in the 1930s, distinctive ties and braiding were introduced for the prefects, and in the summer of 1936 much magazine comment centred on the introduction of boaters instead of school caps. In 1939 it was renamed Moseley Grammar School. It is fair to say, however, that Moseley was less self-consciously elitist than many other selective schools; the 'school song' with a chorus beginning 'Lift up the song of the college on the hill' never seems to have been particularly important, Latin mottoes were not stressed, and the wearing of school uniform seems, from the absence of complaints and occasional references to unusual haircuts, to have been sensibly interpreted.

Pupils in the 1920s were so proud of their uniform that they even wore it on holiday.

Returning to 1923, the first term was summed up in the first edition of The Moseleian thus:

> *We have had a memorable term. No master or boy will forget those early weeks of struggle, when we were engaged in an unequal contest with those untiring gentlemen, the workmen; when it was impossible to hear oneself speak for the banging and clanging outside and in, when it was two boys to a desk and blackboards were rarities. Nor shall we forget the gradual changes as we got to know one another, the arrival of characters, nicknames, a Rugby ball and our acquaintance with the rules of the game, and when we blossomed into school caps, we felt that we had become something more than a mere collection of boys and masters. We esteem ourselves fortunate in our buildings, our beautiful grounds, and particularly in our Headmaster under whose leadership the school will do great things.*

Within a matter of weeks, a tuck shop and a musical society were organised and the first of many concerts given, with plans for a school orchestra in due course; this in fact took another ten years to materialise. Christmas 1925 saw the first dramatic presentation – of Dickens' 'Christmas Carol' – starting a tradition of fine annual performances over the years, often involving boys of all ages and masters as writers, composers, directors and performers. A library was established, with an appeal to boys to donate adventure stories and a

An early but well-remembered production of Toad of Toad Hall.

target of 1,000 volumes within three years, and although the library grew over the years, it contained only 2,000 volumes in 1937 and was heavily criticised when the school was inspected.

A large number of trips out of school were organised. An active Scientific Society included in its programme regular outings to local factories, such as Philip Harris Ltd, Avery's and a brewery, and theatre trips catered for the more literary-minded. The first such outing was to two Shakespeare plays at the Prince of Wales Theatre, which were judged by a young Moseley reviewer to be 'performed very badly', with Macbeth's wild and erratic shouting during the murder scene provoking laughter from the meagre audience.

Two of Moseley's most popular and enduring activities were launched in 1925. First was the formation of the Moseley School Scout Troop (65th Birmingham) under the guidance of Scoutmaster Mr Midgley. Over 75 per cent of the boys applied to join, about half of whom could initially be accepted. What sounds like a rather disastrous meal cooked on a camp fire in the school grounds was reported as the first venture, but by the summer, 41 scouts greatly enjoyed a fortnight's camp on Exmoor. Within two years numbers had so increased that Moseley School had three distinct troops, and a major expedition was under- taken to Switzerland, the first of a number of ambitious overseas expeditions which complemented the annual two-week summer camps in various parts of Britain.

Second was the Literary and Debating Society, offering a programme of talks, debates and mock trials. As the Society got into its stride, the motions chosen for debate give a fascinating glimpse into the topics regarded as interesting or controversial by schoolboys in the 1920s and 30s. There was always a political one, when the conduct of the government was debated, as well as topical issues like rugby versus soccer, talkies versus silent movies and science versus arts subjects. But the most recurring theme seems to have been the opposite sex: 'That the modern girl is degenerate' (1930 – too much powder and paint, said the proposer), 'That the modern girl is inferior to her predecessors' (1934 – 'mob of pro-modern-girlites' prevailed), 'That the absence of ladies on the school staff is regrettable' (1936 – motion defeated, though reality changed in 1939), 'That the fair sex do not deserve that adjective' (1937 – motion carried). Even the Junior Literary and Debating Society, consisting mostly of second formers, diverted from their usual discussions of cycling or sport to debate 'That ladies should always pay for gentlemen'!

Moseley's sporting facilities compared very favourably with those of many other secondary schools; King Edward's Camp Hill, for example, located in the heart of the city until the 1960s, had to travel to playing fields next door to Moseley on what was to become the site of Moseley Modern School. It is not surprising, then, that physical activity received much attention and that the school rapidly gained a formidable reputation in various sporting fields. Mr Gillespie was in charge of Physical Training, but nearly all masters were involved in something – the sporting prowess of many of them suggests that it

An aerial photograph from the 1930s showing the 1920s extension. A cricket hut stands in place of the obelisk. The site below the school was used as playing fields by K.E. Camp Hill. The school is bordered by the 'Dell' and the house Mr Ross built for his family.

was a useful thing to have on one's *curriculum vitae* when applying for a job at Moseley. A Prize Fund was inaugurated, and over the years increasingly complicated arrangements for the sports committee structure and for the allocation of points to determine the award of trophies were loyally reported in The Moseleian.

The playing field in front of the school comfortably accommodated two football pitches, and rugby was the choice, prompting an enthusiastic account in the first school magazine of the initiation into the 'best of all school games' of 'all timid would-be converts from the Soccer game'. (One of those might have been Maths teacher Mr Hill, who captained the Birmingham Amateur Association Football team.) Once the balls had arrived and the posts had been sawn, bolted together and erected by the boys, despite 'their tender years and slender dimensions', training started and house matches got under way. During the Spring Term of 1924, fixtures were played against Yardley Secondary School, Cotteridge Day Continuation School, Central Secondary and Camp Hill Grammar School, resulting in two wins and two defeats.

The rugby tradition at Moseley grew steadily from that first season, with more teams and a full fixture list encompassing all the secondary schools in Birmingham and some further afield – for several years in the 1930s the 'crunch' match was against Burton Grammar School. The school magazine

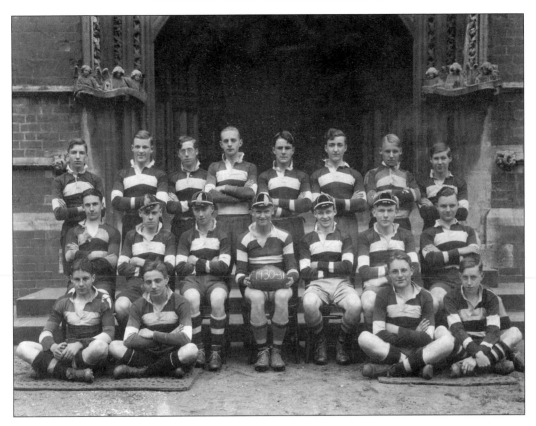

An early team photograph – taken before the angels on either side of the main door were damaged and lost their heads!
The tasselled caps indicated the award of Colours. Leslie Brown, third from right standing, returned to Moseley and served as caretaker for over 20 years.

always carried full reports of the rugby season, reporting the award of colours, half-colours and 'tackling badges', and sometimes including rather merciless analysis of each player's strengths and weaknesses; for example, 'would do better with a greater knowledge of the game', 'lacks enthusiasm off the field' or 'it is regrettable that he should occasionally adopt unorthodox methods in defence'. Teams were coached by enthusiastic masters, and from early days one or two Moseley teachers have periodically appeared in the line-up of Moseley Rugby Football Club.

February 1924 saw over half the school take part in the the first Cross-Country Run, following a 7,000 yard course down Wake Green Road, along the Dingle Walk to Billesley Common, then turning at Yardley Wood Parish Church to return along Yardley Wood Road and Windermere Lane. This became an annual event in which maximum participation was rewarded by a complicated points system, which meant that many boys and some masters completed the run. In 1933 a new course was designed, the old one having become 'cross-town rather than cross-country'; it went from the School across Pickwick Playing Fields, through Swanshurst Park to Yardley Wood Road and Billesley Common, and back again. In due course, some cross-country races were arranged with other schools, though it was not until after the Second World War that a full programme of races was organised.

Moseley Secondary School established an early reputation in athletics. The first full Sports Day in June 1925 was quite an event, with the printing of a special programme and trophies donated by parents and by the Headmaster's wife, who herself was presented with a bouquet by the boys at the close of an afternoon of excitement and glorious sunshine. Fond recollections of Sports Days in the 1960s suggest that the atmosphere changed little over the years. The 1925 programme listed 197 entrants – the entire school – and events consisted of the Mile Team Race, 100 and 220 Yards, the Quarter Mile Handicap, Relay Races, High Jump and Broad Jump, Cricket Ball Throw, Putting the Weight (an eight pound shot), a Tug-of-War and an Obstacle Race which was so popular that it required 18 heats. The winning house, James, celebrated by organising an after school outing by motor-coach to the river at Evesham, returning home at 10.20pm.

Pride was expressed when a few days later, Moseley recorded its first triumph in the Birmingham Inter-Schools Sports as winner of the intermediate relay, which then consisted of six boys running a quarter of a mile each. Just two years later, in 1927, there was great excitement when Moseley won the Kenrick Championship Shield as overall winner of the Inter-School Sports, a remarkable achievement for such a 'young' school competing with fourteen secondary schools. The Shield and four other trophies were proudly displayed on a shelf in the Library. The following year Moseley again won the Shield along with five individual trophies, and thereby established a tradition which meant that Moseley was nearly always a serious contender at the Inter-School Sports.

Cricket took longer to develop successfully, not helped by difficulties in making a decent wicket where the avenue of trees had been. The first season was distinguished by defeats at the hands of King's Norton Secondary School, Hall Green House and Bournville 7th XI, though the school did manage to defeat the Masters' XI by 6 runs. Cricket-loving masters took responsibility for the school teams, which by the 1930s consisted of a 1st XI, a 2nd XI and a Junior XI playing matches against all the local secondary schools. Again, individual criticism of the players sometimes featured in the school magazine and could be all too frank; for example, 'a little too impetuous', 'has a tendency to nibble at the off ball' or 'a bad judge of short runs'.

From 1925, most boys went to the public swimming baths each week, and there were some successes at the Birmingham Inter-School Swimming Sports, though Moseley never excelled at swimming. Mr Gillespie was a firm believer in physical fitness (he himself lived to the age of 105), and his chief enthusiasms were for boxing and gymnastics. The former was actively pursued at Moseley, with internal competitions and occasional fixtures against other schools. A regular and popular feature at the end of each Summer Term from 1933 was the Field Gymnastic Demonstration, which included physical training displays, mass exercises, vaulting, self defence and a ' chariot race'.

An interesting item in many of these programmes was dancing. The inclusion as a surprise item in the school concert of Easter 1934 of seven boys performing the Kirby sword dance produced such rapturous applause that similar routines became a regular feature for a time. The 1937 school concert included a 'rather startling innovation' in the shape of a School Ballet, when costumes instead of gym kit were worn to perform the Highland Fling, the Irish Jig and the Sailor's Hornpipe, followed by 'Athletic Poses of the Fifth and Sixth Forms', when 'new lighting devices produced a series of pictures which will long be remembered'! Finally, on the sporting front, it is worth noting that Moseley staff had a fine record of success in the golf tournament for 'Masters teaching at Secondary Schools in Birmingham and District' inaugurated in 1928.

Of course, achievement in sport and other activities improved as the school grew bigger and the boys in it older and stronger. The annual intake of new boys increased from 100 to 120 in September 1927, and for many years each individual arrival and departure was recorded in the Salvete and Valete column of The Moseleian, a practice which was discontinued only on the outbreak of the Second World War. Compared with today, however, it was a changing school population. The school leaving age was 14 and although secondary schools were supposed to keep their pupils at least until the Fifth form and the School Certificate Examination (the forerunner of GCSE), there was much less of an established pattern of staying to the Sixth form and higher education than became the norm at grammar schools later in the century.

The high unemployment of the 1930s encouraged a number of boys to seek and accept jobs rather than continue their education, and the school magazine often bid farewell to senior pupils leaving in the middle of the school year or even during term-time. The careers they went on to included accountancy, administrative posts, engineering, teaching and the civil and armed services. The school roll was also affected from time to time by the death of a pupil – more frequently, it seems, than today but clearly just as distressing.

The departure of most of the first intake of boys in the summer of 1927 was a poignant moment for the school. The school magazine echoed Mr Robinson in paying tribute to 'those hardy veterans' who had done so much to establish certain Moseley traditions, chief of which were good sportsmanship and physical fitness. Of the original 99 boys who began in 1923, 42 were entered for School Certificate four years later, of whom 26 passed, 13 at matriculation standard. This modest academic record was duly acknowledged, with exhortations to improve. A small number progressed to the Sixth form and just five succeeded in gaining their Higher School Certificate (A Level equivalent) in 1929. Three of those became Moseley's first university entrants.

The departure of the main cohort prompted the formation of an Old Boys' Society, warmly encouraged by Mr Robinson. It immediately devised a tie in the same colours as the school's, launched a rugby team and planned some social activities. Thus began half a century of the Old Moseleians, a period of fluctuating fortunes in terms of support and sporting success. After a nomadic start, the Society was delighted to secure a rugby pitch at Windermere Road and a room in the United Services Club, which facilitated close relationships with the school, including a series of successful dances.

Indeed, contact and co-operation were often closer than would be thought possible today, with Old Boys playing in the school orchestra for concerts, attending gymnastic and swimming classes and even rugby training run by masters from the school, and constantly being urged to support school functions. It is worth remembering that many of the Old Boys were, initially at least, just 15 or 16 years of age and making their way in the world of work, and no doubt glad of the continuing contact with their school colleagues. This could not have been more true than during the Second World War.

The War brought radical change to Moseley School as to every other part of national life. An awareness of European affairs was evident from the mid-1930s onwards, with The Moseleian adopting an increasingly sombre tone. From a rather flippant editorial in 1936 – 'If Hitler can shout 'Heil Hitler' in the Unter den Linden then the School can shout 'School' in the last Rugby match of the season' – to a naïve Sixth Former describing his 1937 trip to Berlin: 'I was most impressed by Hitler's progress in beautifying Berlin' – and a visiting German boy observing in 1938 that 'your Scout movement appears to be very much like our Hitler Youth Movement', a Sixth Former wrote seriously in March 1939 that 'the shadow of war seemed to hang like a pall over the school'. He reported that nearly all the staff had volunteered for the Fire Service and anti-aircraft duties, necessitating their absence from school on occasions, and he blamed the Government for not providing adequately 'for an event such as seemed likely to envelope Europe in its holocaust'.

By Christmas 1939, more than half the school had been evacuated to Cheltenham. Summoned back early from their summer holidays, the boys and several of the masters had just one day's notice of the evacuation, and on 1 September travelled by train with the party from King Edward's Girls' High School. War was declared on 3 September. Moseley seems to have been more fortunate in its destination than were many evacuees, for the arrangements were efficient and the welcome warm; as Mr Hughes, in charge of the party, commented, 'One must feel admiration and thanks for the manner in which the work was done. We express our appreciation and thanks to those people of Cheltenham who have given such willing service'. The boys then effectively had three weeks' holiday in glorious weather, before classes began on 22 September sharing Cheltenham Grammar School's accommodation.

Considering the disruption to normal procedures, school life continued fairly uneventfully. Moseley boys were taught on alternate days, with plenty of Rugby and spare time in between, some of which was occupied by the newly-founded Film Society. The Scouts continued, as did the Literary and Debating

Society, and Sundays became renowned for Mr Smith's hikes following a religious service. The most popular aspect of life in Cheltenham seems to have been the 'drippers' or dripping cakes served at break; the least popular 'the most unbearable smell' from the next-door brewery.

Christmas 1939 saw most boys back in Birmingham and Moseley School reopened for voluntary attendance in January 1940. Numbers increased to around 350 by the end of term, when the Cheltenham evacuation officially terminated, and the temporary stay of King Edward's Grammar School, Camp Hill, in Moseley's building came to an end. Workmen arrived to erect air-raid shelters, but by late 1940 concern for Birmingham children's safety returned and on 26 November, 82 boys and five masters from Moseley School were evacuated again, this time to King Charles I Grammar School at Kidderminster.

Just two days later, during a raid which affected a number of homes in the Moseley area, four bombs fell on Moseley School. Two landed on the field, making craters, a third damaged the West Wing and a fourth did considerable damage to the Science Wing and the Dining Hall. An observer wrote: 'Internally, the School reminded one of the China shop after the bull had left. Broken glass was everywhere, while in the Science wing, doors and window frames had been hurled many yards.' The school had to close for ten days and full repairs wait until the end of the War, but with a depleted school – about 260 boys – still in Birmingham, the eleven serviceable rooms sufficed for the time being. A few days later, incendiary bombs fell on the building and a serious fire in the Gymnasium was prevented only by the prompt action of one of the masters.

By October 1941, all but 35 boys and two masters had left Kidderminster, and by the summer of 1942 they too had returned to Moseley, which then had 482 on the school roll. It was to reach 563 the following year. Some forms were substantially under strength; VI A Lit, for example, consisted of just one boy (J.L. Sheppard, who made his cricketing reputation at this time, before going to Cambridge University in 1943), and even in normal years, the Literary Sixth form was always very much smaller than the Science Sixth. Distinctive wartime activities included the founding of a well-supported Cadet Corps and War Savings Group, and attendance at an annual Harvest Camp. From 1943, incidentally, the School Magazine appeared without a cover because of the shortage of card, a situation which lasted until 1952.

Most significantly, of course, many Moseleians were actively involved in the War. Some of the staff joined up, while the rest were busy in the Home Guard (of which Mr Robinson was South Birmingham Brigadier) or the Wardens. In 1941 Moseley School welcomed its first females to the staff in the shape of two 21 year old graduate-trained teachers, the first of some 15 women who taught at Moseley during the War years. Some stayed only a few months; others became quite well established, one of whom provided the 'piece de resistance' of the Debating Society's 1943 programme when she 'convinced the majority of her audience that the sooner Co-education was introduced here at Moseley, the better for everybody.' In all, there were 31 staff appointments between 1940 and 1947, only six of whom were still in post at the latter date.

Former pupils were much in everyone's minds. Given the date of the school's foundation, every Old Moseleian was of an age to serve and it is estimated that 1,300 did. They seem to have favoured the Air Force but all possible branches of the armed services were noted. As a former soldier himself, Mr Robinson seems to have been particularly solicitous for his Old Boys' welfare, and the school magazine became a focus for news, recording information about postings and promotions and being despatched all over the world to any Moseleian of whom the school had knowledge. Sadly, the news all too often included the annotation 'Killed in action' and by the end of the War, 93 Moseleians had lost their lives.

A memorial fund set up in 1946 under the supervision of three bereaved parents, three members of the school and three Old Boys, led to the unveiling, in 1950, of the War Memorial in the school's entrance hall. It was decided to list names and initials only, and not rank or decorations. Made of bronze and set in a surround of Caen stone, the Memorial was dedicated by the Vicar of Moseley at a service attended by a large number of parents, and is now being used again for commemorative services.

After the War, school life gradually returned to normal, though it is not always appreciated that the return to normality in many spheres of national life took some years, certainly until the early 1950s. There were significant changes in education, with the post-war implementation of the 1944 Act which introduced free secondary education for all 11-15 year olds. The grammar schools, seen as beacons of excellence and allowed to continue their privileged existence, were little touched by the Act, though fee-paying parents (probably the minority at Moseley by 1945) no doubt appreciated the ending of fees and charges for text books.

Birmingham, like all other local authorities, was primarily concerned with providing for the unselected majority of children. Moseley Grammar School's new neighbour, Moseley Modern School, was one of the more positive results. This was also the time (1951) when the General Certificate of Education replaced the old School Certificate, and The Moseleian annually listed successes in the new examinations. It has to be said that some of the lists, particularly the 15-20 names at Advanced level, were not as long as might be expected from a school taking well over a hundred selected boys each year. His Majesty's Inspectors, who scrutinised the school in 1948, evidently agreed that academic standards should be higher and criticised the teachers for a 'widespread failure to extend the pupils'. Mr Robinson submitted a formal response defending his staff, drawing attention to the difficulties of the War period and presenting figures to show that standards in 1947-8 were higher than in 1939. The 'falling standards' debate has always been a difficult one to prove!

Wartime wear and tear to the Moseley building was repaired by the end of 1948, and during 1953-4 more technical rooms and a dining hall were added in a new block whose style shows all too clearly the austerity of the times. Some new members of staff were welcomed and new activities launched, notably the Field Club in 1947, while older societies got going again and the Cadet Corps continued to flourish. It was also a sparkling time for musical productions under the inspirational guidance of Stanley Adams. Inter-school sports were re-established by 1948-9 and Moseley's sporting record seems, if anything, to have been enhanced by the interruption of war. Pupil Bob Stolz played Rugby for England, and in 1954 Moseley regained the Kenrick Shield for athletics, starting a remarkable run of six consecutive victories, including a record points total in 1956.

1st Violin—Tobias, L. Smith, H. E. Paynes, H. V. Lumby, J. R. Payne, R. F. Seager, W. J. Betts. A.   2nd Violin—Mr. S. C. N. Smith
Staples, G. L. Robinson, J. P. Haynes, J. Horton, R. W.   Cellos— Mr. C. K. Brampton. Royston, J. R   Bass— Mr. J. R. Ward
Recorders—Hunt. W. J. White, A. J.   Oboe—Mr. Reeves.   Clarinets—Mr. Morley. Marshall, D. P. Harris, G. P.   Trumpets—
Hodgetts. B. F. Nunn, H. B.   Euphoniums—Whyley, A. G. Longshaw, R. G.   Horn—Lane, M. C.   Trombone—Hancock, A. G
Tubas—Booth, P. J. Bellamy, P. D. Tympani—Paynes, B. V. Side Drum—Bracey, D. H. Bass Drum—Hack, R. C. Piano—Massey, R. C

The school orchestra for a 'Festival of Britain' concert in 1951. The conductor was the legendary Mr Stanley Adams. The pianist, Roy Massey, went on to a distinguished career as a Cathedral organist.

A number of stalwart staff came to the end of their careers in the immediate post-war years. Mrs Moore, who had run the Canteen since the school's opening, retired, receiving particular thanks from the school games teams. Mr Jones, in charge of Handicraft since 1923, had postponed his retirement for five years to help the school, and his death soon afterwards was sadly noted. Another of the 'originals', Mr Andrews, died suddenly in 1953 while still in post, and Mr Robinson himself suffered an extended illness during 1951-2. He was in his sixties by then and his impending retirement prompted two senior colleagues – Deputy Head Mr Hughes and Senior English Master Mr Keyte – to close their careers after thirty years each at Moseley School. It was indeed the end of an era.

Creating a new school is always something of a challenge, even in these days when there are rules and guidelines to cover so many aspects of school life. In the 1920s, when much more reliance was placed on the professional wisdom of headteachers and their staffs, it must have presented an exhilarating opportunity to the small band of young men who launched Moseley Secondary School. The school which they shaped, under the guidance of Mr Robinson, established an impressive record of achievement and a fine reputation in the city of Birmingham, yet most importantly is referred to as a thoroughly happy school.

Mr Robinson – perhaps selected for the organisational and personal skills he had demonstrated so effectively in his war service – proved to be a fine leader. He was resilient, calm, cheerful and unfailingly courteous. A good listener with a formidable memory, he stored away details about all his boys and staff so that he could always greet them in a friendly fashion. He believed strongly in teamwork, co-operation and loyalty, and his discretion and absence of favouritism were said to have imbued the whole staff with a sense of security:

> *At the farewell dinner given to our headmaster, not a single chair was empty. If other schools can show this unanimity, they are as fortunate as they are few.*

References and acknowledgements

This chapter draws heavily on the virtually complete set of The Moseleian magazines held in the school archive and meticulously catalogued by Roy Holloway. Supporting evidence comes from File ED35/6312 (Moseley Secondary School) in the Public Record Office; from various Committee Minutes and newspaper reports in the Archives section of the Birmingham Central Library; and from the official History of the Corporation of Birmingham (several volumes, various years). Our thanks to John Sheppard for his personal reminiscences, to P.R. Pickard and Margaret Yarnall (nee Brown) for the loan of photographs and to Birmingham Design Services for the loan of architects' drawings.

Chapter Five

Moseley Modern School 1955-1972

Moseley Modern School owed its official existence to the 1944 Education Act, though the thinking behind the post-war reforms dates back to the 1920s and 1930s when a series of influential government reports wrestled with the problem of how to provide a more worthwhile education for older elementary schoolchildren. A consensus emerged that primary education should cease at 11, at which point children would move on to one of three types of secondary school: grammar for a minority of children who are 'interested in learning for its own sake'; technical for those who have 'uncanny insights into the intricacies of mechanism'; and modern for the majority (75-80 per cent) who 'deal more easily with concrete things than with ideas, who are interested only in the moment and are essentially practical'. The more progressive local authorities, like Birmingham, had already followed this lead and gone a considerable way towards developing better opportunities for children over 11 in its creation of 'senior mixed departments', as at College Road.

The tripartite system rested on the confident assertion of psychologists that each child's intelligence quotient was an inherited and fixed commodity which could be tested as part of the 11-plus examination. As one historian has wryly observed, 'the suggestion seems to be that the Almighty has benevolently created three types of child in just those proportions which would justify educational administrators'.

It is difficult for anyone who has not experienced the system to appreciate the monumental significance of the 11-plus. Primary schools had to concentrate on streaming and drilling their young pupils for the examination, and parents very quickly became aware of the importance of success. One primary teacher recorded that inducements offered to her top class to pass the 11-plus included sixteen new bicycles, three watches, three puppies, a bedroom clock, a portable radio, a tennis racket, a perm, and a pair of roller skates!

The Birmingham Education Committee indicated its own reservations about the system when it undertook a major review of the Secondary Schools Admission Examination in 1954, just before Moseley Modern School opened. It discussed all the worrying features of 11-plus selection – such as the inevitable margin of error, fairness to borderline candidates, the drawback of a 'snap' decision on a child's long-term potential – and reported that there were then places in maintained grammar schools for just 14 per cent of the city's children plus some at the King Edward's Schools. Clearly, there was enormous scope for the new secondary modern schools, despite the constraints imposed on them, to develop a worthwhile style of education for the remainder.

Official government pronouncements were emphatic that secondary modern schools should develop a distinctive ethos and curriculum: 'free from the pressures of any external examination, these schools can work out the best and liveliest forms of secondary education suited to their pupils.' There was talk of 'generous expenditure' and 'parity of conditions with other types of secondary school', which would enable secondary modern schools to build their own reputations and convince parents of their worth.

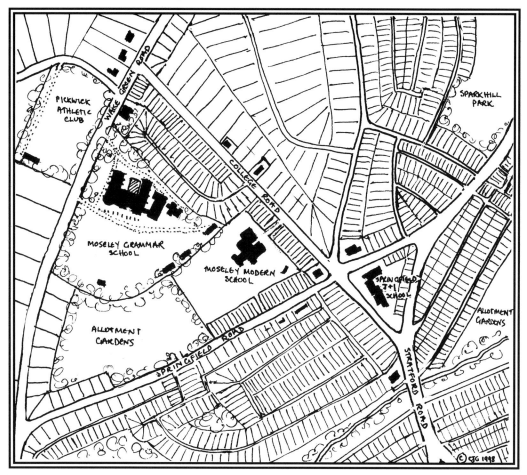

By the late 1950s the area was almost completely built up. It was now served by three schools, as Moseley Modern replaced the senior school at College Road which, in turn, was renamed Springfield Junior and Infants School.

Moseley Modern Mixed School did not have an easy start. There had been serious problems with the construction work. The name 'Springhill' turned out to be only too appropriate and the building had to be constructed on concrete rafts. It was not ready for the opening of the new school. The 776 pupils and 28 staff had to manage with ten classes in the new school, seven in the old school, three in St Christopher's Annexe and one 'travelling class'. Two classes consisted of girls who were waiting to be transferred to the new Swanshurst Grammar School when it was finished. The first day of term was spent by the staff and some specially selected pupils in unpacking and making lists of the stock but the school was by no means fully equipped and throughout the first term there were frequent visits from the Local Authority's advisers. By November, however, trees and shrubs were being planted in the school garden and in February the school closed for two days to complete the move into the new building, most of which was now finished. St Christopher's Annexe had been in use for ten years in all!

1955. Moseley Modern Mixed School

All the existing staff transferred from College Road, with Miss Eileen Cohen as Head, and there were several new appointments. The first recorded staff absence was on the second day of the first term and this continued to be a problem. One former member of staff recalls with feeling that 'supply teachers had not been invented' and remembers 'doubling up' on many occasions. The Log Book records in March of one year that it was only the third day since the previous September that the full staff had been present.

As with all secondary modern schools, there were also problems filling staff vacancies in spite of the school's growing reputation. Before the end of the first year departing staff had not been replaced and this situation is clearly reflected in a meeting of secondary modern school Heads with the Chief Education Officer to 'discuss the staffing crisis'. A comparison with the number of applicants for many posts in grammar schools shows clearly their perceived status. The General Inspection report in 1959 commented that there had been 40 staff changes in four years and at the start of one term, ten newly qualified teachers began on the same day.

Moseley Modern School is an austere building with none of the decorative flourishes of its predecessor, College Road School.

Nonetheless, the school was seen as a model of its kind as evidenced by the number of important visitors it received. As well as the Chairman of the Education Committee, who arrived one evening, asked to be shown over the school and finally left at 10.20, there were frequent parties of civic dignitaries and inspectors, students from Russia, teachers and education experts from America, Australia and the West Indies.

Miss Cohen had a very clear vision of the kind of school she wanted and put her views with equal firmness whether dealing with pupils in school or explaining the school's requirements to the Chief Education Officer. She represented the school and the city on a number of educational bodies and was considered a formidable figure. A former colleague comments that 'Miss Cohen gave such a clear lead and had such a strong personality that punishment was not much needed'. He recalls her stubbing out her cigarette and marching out of her smoke-filled study to berate a group of boys who had been caught smoking! The General Inspection Report of 1959 refers to the way 'her warm and generous personality pervades the school' and describes her as a 'good leader and organiser'. Her commitment to the school was total; she frequently worked in school for weeks of the summer holiday and returned to school from hospital on one occasion 'unofficially' with her leg in plaster and 'forbidden to put it to the ground'.

The style was traditional; there was a uniform and a school badge, houses and prefects and strict discipline. Mrs Margaret Yarnall (nee Brown) was one of the pupils chosen to help with the move to the new school. She remembers 'you were not allowed to run anywhere on the premises and ... you were not allowed to even talk as you walked across the main entrance'. Assembly took place first thing every morning and 'if anything upset the Head we were all back there after school to do the whole thing again'. She agrees that relatively little punishment was needed as 'staff and pupils were all proud of their new school' and 'the atmosphere was a very happy one'. Corporal punishment continued to be used, albeit sparingly, until 1971. Most instances of caning were for smoking and truancy in the early years; later the cane was used for 'disobedience' and 'insolence'.

Academically, the school began well, although all its pupils had 'failed' the 11-plus. Its intake came mainly from Sparkhill which was in those days a close-knit and very supportive community with high expectations of its children. In its first year, 800 parents attended the Open Evening and Speech Days were major events. Pupils were firmly streamed from the start; there was a GCE class, a number of Technical and Commercial classes, a 'Homemakers' class and a 'Basic' class. From the beginning, many pupils stayed on beyond the compulsory Leaving Age to complete their fifth year, although it was possible to leave at Christmas and Easter as well as in July, and a successful sixth form was also soon established.

A class in the late 1950's with Deputy Head Mr Higgins.

By the time of the General Inspection in 1959 a second GCE class had been created for pupils wishing to take the examination in selected subjects. There were by then over 900 pupils of whom 92 were in the fifth year and 18 in the sixth. This was in a building designed for 600 and necessitated the use of three rooms on the old College Road site as well as classes being taught in the former sports pavilion, the hall, library, medical room, staffroom and dining room. The report commented approvingly that 'during one lunch hour forty pupils were observed reading and looking at books in a most orderly manner'. It concluded that 'this lively, interesting school has established itself quickly and soundly in new buildings despite the difficulties created by excessive numbers and frequent changes of staff'.

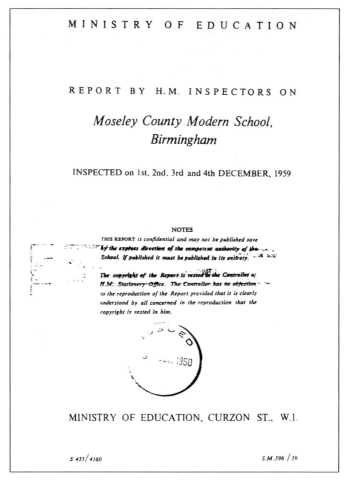

MINISTRY OF EDUCATION

REPORT BY H.M. INSPECTORS ON

Moseley County Modern School,
Birmingham

INSPECTED on 1st, 2nd, 3rd and 4th DECEMBER, 1959

NOTES

THIS REPORT *is confidential and may not be published save*
by the express direction of the competent authority of the
School. If published it must be published in its entirety.

The copyright of the Report is vested in the Controller of
H.M. Stationery Office. The Controller has no objection
to the reproduction of the Report provided that it is clearly
understood by all concerned in the reproduction that the
copyright is vested in him.

ISSUED
1950

MINISTRY OF EDUCATION, CURZON ST., W.1.

S 455/4160   S.M.396 / 59

The General Inspection report, just four years after the school opened. It was a much
less elaborate performance than an Ofsted inspection today.

The full programme of cultural visits which had been developed at College Road continued. On the same day in October 1956 a large party went to 'The Merry Wives of Windsor' at the then Stratford Memorial Theatre while another group went to a concert of classical music in the Town Hall. Four days later there was another large theatre party. A tradition of successful concerts and productions began.

The school also continued to develop its sporting reputation, winning almost every trophy for team sport in the city. This, despite having to 'build their own jumping pit – the work of a group of boys under Mr Scott' and having to walk to Colebank playing fields for games lessons – a distance that would exhaust many of the present generation before they even got there! In all these activities there was enthusiastic staff participation, whether in closely fought staff versus pupils sports fixtures or in memorable performances of Gilbert and Sullivan.

Early success for the school's football team. Mr Scott, who built up the sporting reputation, is on the left, the Headmistress, Miss Cohen, is in the centre and Mr Lockwood, who went on to become Deputy Head, is on the right.

By the time Miss Cohen (by then Mrs North) retired in 1967, things were beginning to change. There was growing discontent in many quarters with the selection of children at the age of eleven, both in principle and in practice. Although Moseley Modern had begun in much more favourable circumstances than many secondary modern schools, which had simply taken over the buildings of former council schools, it was nonetheless poorly equipped, funded and staffed compared with every grammar school in the city. The question of comprehensive schools had become a political issue, especially in Birmingham, where the situation was further complicated by the special status of the King Edward Foundation Schools. It would be nearly ten years before Birmingham finally completed its comprehensive reorganisation but the 1965 directive to Local Authorities had put the question firmly on the national agenda and most of those working in education knew that the change would come.

Other developments affected Moseley Modern School during this period. Firstly, the School Leaving Age was raised and all non-selective schools were faced with the challenge of providing for and motivating pupils who would not previously have chosen to stay on. Secondly, the school's catchment area began changing in character. Many old-established families started to move further away from the city centre into the greener suburbs and Sparkhill became home to a more rapidly changing population. A significant percentage of the school's intake now came from families who were recently arrived in Britain and needed extra help to settle in.

The newly appointed Head was Mr Donald Wilford. His style was very different as the changing educational climate required. Several teachers who worked under him have commented on his tremendous commitment to helping pupils with problems (and their parents). The Log Book records long meetings, sometimes lasting all evening, spent trying to resolve the behaviour problems of certain pupils. One colleague remembers him 'taking the social misfits of the school under his wing' and liking nothing better than 'getting out on the playground and throwing a rugby ball around with some of the lads'. The curriculum continued to encourage most pupils to aim for at least six CSEs and/or O Levels. The most able could take seven or eight and the least able between one and five. The Sixth Form offered 14 A Level subjects and 26 O Levels. The school became more child-centred and began developing a formal pastoral system and activity periods.

These developments allowed the school to maintain its consistent academic record. In 1968 there were 750 CSE grades 1 and 2 and the A Level results improved constantly. The commitment to sporting and musical success was also remarkable; ten sporting trophies were won that same year and by the 1970s the school was running three choirs, a wind band, several music groups and a developing string section. One former teacher describes this as 'the time of extra-curricular activities supreme'. There were trips to local and foreign destinations, school plays, musicals and a huge range of sporting opportunities in which 'vast numbers took part'. At one point there were 67 sports teams! Mr Wilford and Mr Lockwood, who was appointed as Deputy Head in 1969 and is remembered as 'he of the photographic memory', dealt with the problems created by a less stable social climate without suspending a single pupil of statutory school age.

The school's sporting success was not limited to team trophies. The tradition of excellence inherited from College Road, which produced the Tokyo Olympic steeplechase silver medallist, Maurice Herriot, was continued by Daphne Arden (later Daphne Slater) a sprint bronze medallist in Tokyo and by Sharon Corbett who won a Commonwealth bronze medal in the javelin in 1974. Steve Rouse, after several seasons with Warwickshire, is now established as Head Groundsman at Edgbaston. Nisar Chauhdry played hockey for England while Noel Luke and Mickey Lewis made successful careers as professional footballers.

The school continued to be shown to visitors from all over the world as well as to groups of local teachers. But there was never any doubt that the neighbouring grammar schools were better funded, better staffed and better equipped in every way. John Lockwood recalls that even the soap and towels provided for the staff were a different colour! As Local Authorities around the country began moving in large numbers towards comprehensive reorganisation, the pressure on large authorities like Birmingham, which had traditionally been at the forefront of progressive educational thinking, was growing.

In the meantime, the school's most pressing problem was one of space. Building extensions first discussed in October 1970 were not finished by January 1974 and there were by now nearly 1,000 pupils on roll. Two second year classes had to be taught at the Grammar School and two classes of fourth year girls at the Sparkhill Centre. Mrs Betty Gillespie has vivid memories of this:

> *I moved to Moseley Mixed School as Head of Business Studies in September 1972, and had one very large room, one large empty stock room (which held 12 pupils) and a landing! We were waiting for the new wing to be completed. In September 1973, the new wing was still not ready for occupation and so the department was temporarily housed at Sparkhill Institute on the Stratford Road, with two members of staff based there, and one left at College Road.*

Other lessons took place on the stage, in the pavilion and in the boys' cloakroom. The staff managed to alleviate some of the stress and uncertainty of the situation by organising a four-day staff trip to Benidorm before the start of term in January!

In fact staff 'camaraderie' is a striking feature of this period and must have contributed to the generally optimistic approach to the proposed amalgamation with Moseley Grammar School, despite the doubts described by Betty Gillespie:

> *I don't think anyone on the staff welcomed this, and we hoped until almost the end of the Summer term that it would never happen. However, it became apparent at the public meeting that the decision had actually been made, and nothing anyone could say in opposition was going to have the slightest effect on the outcome. I would say the feeling of staff at Moseley Mixed at that point was one of frustration, but ultimately, of course, they became resigned to the situation.*

Although there were many uncertainties ahead the approach was fairly relaxed; secondary modern teachers had learned over the years to become adaptable and to expect a less than ideal situation. Amalgamation was seen mainly in terms of the opportunities a large comprehensive would bring. As John Lockwood memorably put it 'we thought we might all get white soap!'

Moseley Modern School is a fascinating case study of the secondary modern school system: the rationale and aspirations behind its introduction, and the limitations prescribed for it which in time exposed the inherent flaws in the system. Where conditions were favourable – new buildings could be financed and a good staff put in place – secondary modern schools achieved as much as anyone could have hoped of them. Unfortunately, they were disadvantaged in all sorts of ways compared with grammar schools. The manner in which school finances were calculated provided a lot more money for older pupils, which the secondary modern schools did not have, so they were short of books, resources and equipment, and less able to attract well-qualified teachers. And many of their pupils were not easy to teach, because they saw themselves as 'failures', and because the schools could provide no particular goal or qualification at which to aim.

Over time, as schools got into their stride, attitudes to both of these drawbacks changed. By the late 1950s it became clear that the majority of secondary modern schools were, despite official disapproval, entering some of their pupils for external examinations, such as those of the Royal Society of Arts and the General Nursing Council as well as the General Certificate of Education. The fact that they were doing rather well led to the introduction of the Certificate of Secondary Education from 1965, as well as fuelling the growing criticism of the 11-plus examination as a means of sorting and labelling children and effectively determining their futures.

With its favourable catchment area, smart new building and some very committed teachers, Moseley Modern probably achieved as much as any secondary modern school could have and must, by any measure, rank as one of the most successful examples of its kind.

References and acknowledgements

This chapter draws heavily on the School's Log Book, the only official document in the school to have survived the flooding of the building. Further information is held by the Local Studies section of the Birmingham Central Library. Our thanks to John Lockwood, Steve Rosson, Betty Gillespie and Brian Miles for their memories and to Margaret Yarnall (nee Brown) for reminiscences and photographs.

Chapter Six

Moseley Grammar School 1955-1972

One year after the establishment of Moseley Modern School, Moseley Grammar School was adjusting to life under a new Head. It must have been something of a culture shock. Mr Robinson had finally retired in December 1955 just short of his 66th birthday; Mr D.B. Gaskin was twenty years younger, although he had already been Head of Henry Thornton Grammar School in London for six years. He had been educated at Liverpool College where he won an Open Scholarship to read History at Oxford. He was a keen sportsman and had played tennis for Shropshire.

Mr D.B. Gaskin, Headmaster 1956-1972

He brought with him a young family for whom the main shock was not living in a boys' school but moving from a normal house into 15 large and freezing rooms. The school's central heating had not been extended to the Headmaster's House, which was the only one of its kind in the city. This situation continued for seven years until a large deputation from the Architects Department visited the school in the bitter winter of 1962 to draw up plans for a new science block and, as it later emerged, a new school. Mrs Gaskin kindly offered them coffee. The visitors politely declined to remove their overcoats as their coffee turned stone-cold, their hands went numb and their breath froze in the air; the following week engineers arrived to measure up for central heating.

Mr Gaskin took over a school with much in its favour. The building was still a landmark, despite beginning to show its age. There were many very experienced members of staff, including eleven who had been appointed in the school's first decade – a remarkable record. In the main, they accepted the arrival of a new Head with equanimity. The school had an enviable sporting record and a good reputation in the city. It was always oversubscribed despite a four-form entry, rising to five forms on several occasions, with 35 in each class. These numbers put constant pressure on the accommodation and lessons were taught in some very strange places.

Its most striking quality, however, was its happy atmosphere. Mr Robinson had been a much-loved Headmaster, inspiring affection and loyalty. Mr Gaskin was his preferred choice of the candidates interviewed to succeed him and he

Mr Gaskin inherited a somewhat larger staff than the
seven who had started under Mr Robinson.

was warmly welcomed. He, in turn, was conscious of the need to introduce changes gradually and tactfully. So much so that Mr Brampton, one of the original members of staff and then Deputy Head commented on 'the surprise we experience when we bring ourselves to believe that he has already been with us a whole year, and we begin to wonder what is new about him'.

But there were important changes to be made. The 1956 examination results showed barely 20 per cent of pupils (all of them selected by the 11-plus) gaining five or more GCEs. Such a statistic today would certainly bring the wrath of OFSTED down on the school! Mr J.L. Sheppard who had been a pupil at the school from 1937 to 1943 and returned in 1956 as a teacher, was in a position to comment that 'Mr Gaskin was a much more "hands on" Head than his predecessor' which 'was necessary in order to raise standards of achievement; the increasing success in terms of examination success, first choice entrants and public regard over the years was due to staff as well as Head but Mr Gaskin was the catalyst'. So what exactly changed?

Certainly the academic side of school life was given a higher profile. The most visible innovation was the school's first ever Speech Day and Prize Giving held in September 1956 at which Mr Gaskin praised every aspect of the school but also explained some important changes. There was now to be a separate Junior School comprising the First and Second Forms with its own Head, Mr Starling, and later Mr Bullock, and its own accommodation. Teachers were

ELEVATION TO WAKE GREEN ROAD.

The outward appearance of west wing had been changed by the 1920s conversion work. Chimneys and the turret were removed and the central doorway became a window. Floor levels were altered to give classrooms the required height. This became the Junior wing when Mr Gaskin established the Junior School in 1956.

encouraged to teach at least two subjects to the junior forms 'to ease the transition from primary school'. Junior school prefects from the Lower Sixth were 'carefully chosen for their ability to combine good discipline with a sympathetic understanding of the problems of new boys'. Competitions for work were introduced alongside the traditional sporting ones as well as a junior magazine and a Festival of Arts. Many innovations were ahead of their time and would seem familiar to teachers and pupils in the 1990s. Each boy was issued with an individual record book for homework and assessment and each class had a form diary recording effort and behaviour in every lesson.

Speech Days were initially held in the Friends' Meeting House in Moseley Road but soon outgrew the building as more and more parents attended. From 1961 the school filled the Town Hall each year. Mr Gaskin's address attracted increasing media attention as his, and the school's, reputation grew. He used the occasion to report in detail on the full range of achievements of groups and individuals but also to comment forcefully on current educational issues, as in 1962 when he attacked the failure to provide more university and college places as 'not only disastrously short-sighted, but also a betrayal of the legitimate hopes and ambitions of some of the best of our young people'. In 1966 he took issue with a report claiming that public schools did better than maintained ones by proving that Moseley Grammar School actually outperformed them all.

The emphasis on work obviously extended to all age groups and by 1959 the number of boys obtaining five or more GCEs had risen to 50 per cent. Mr Gaskin introduced other changes more gradually. The aims of the curriculum were now to provide 'equal opportunities for the more gifted and the less' and to devise a five-year course that was 'complete in itself, an adequate preparation for earning a living but also a foundation for good citizenship'. This embodied his belief that those who did not go on to A Levels and university were of equal value, an approach further illustrated by the subsequent phasing out of rigid streaming. Years 1 and 2 were taught in 'equal ability classes' moving on into broad ability bands before being 'set' for some subjects at GCE level. In the late 1950s and early 1960s these were unusual measures for a grammar school to take.

Several new subjects were introduced throughout the school, such as Spanish, Russian and Technical Drawing, but the biggest change was to the Sixth Form curriculum. The trend towards increasing specialisation was countered and the rigid separation between arts and sciences was broken down. General Studies, Music and Art Appreciation, Current Affairs, PE and Games were taken by all, as were practical periods of either Art or Handicraft. Scientists had a period of English Literature and of Russian and linguists had to do some General Science. All this reflected the Head's own breadth of learning.

Other changes had less predictable results. The school was in serious need of redecoration and work was begun in the first summer holiday. When the staff entered the hall for the first assembly of the new school year, they found a sea of upturned faces – engaged not in divine adoration, but in close study of the naked nymphs on the ceiling which had been previously hidden by years of accumulated dirt and were now picked out in two tasteful colours! Typically, Mr Gaskin offered a prize to the boy who could correctly identify the Greek legends depicted.

The culture of the school was also changing, almost imperceptibly. Like most grammar schools of its time, it had been modelled on the English public school with great emphasis on the house system and many decisions in the hands of the four house masters. The reward system had also tended to create small academic or sporting elites with special privileges. A more egalitarian structure was now developed with opportunities for more individuals to succeed; prizes were awarded across a wide spectrum of activities and the XL Club extended recognition of achievement to many more boys.

A School Council was formed and, more unusually, the Head implemented many of its recommendations. At Speech Days for example, prizes for a few were replaced with certificates for many, boys were allowed to sit with their parents and guest speakers were dispensed with. Rigid uniform rules were relaxed and many potential problems resolved by negotiation. In fact, Moseley and its liberal Head were frequently quoted in the local press during the sixties as other schools hit the headlines in disputes over the length of hair, the wearing of caps or the pointedness of shoes!

Whilst no school could claim to be free of bullying, it does not appear to have been a dominant feature of life at Moseley. The cane was then the main disciplinary sanction in almost all schools. Mr Gaskin made it clear that he did not support corporal punishment but allowed a few senior colleagues to use the cane for a transitional period. As it was phased out, with no deterioration in the orderliness of the school, the consensus among the boys was that a quick caning would have been preferable to the Head's favoured approach – an in-depth discussion in his office of their motives, their behaviour and its consequences. A number of other rituals came to an abrupt end with Mr Gaskin's arrival, such as the end of term anarchy which had led to an unpopular master being trussed up and locked in a cupboard and another having his car pushed into the middle of the field and its wheels removed.

Many of the original staff were reaching retiring age and left, frequently after careers spent entirely at Moseley. One or two were not happy with the direction the school was now taking and chose to go. A number of new members of staff were also Old Moseleians. Mr Graham Bate recalls being one of five in the early 1960s, adding 'I am not sure if this was a measure of our enjoyment of the school when pupils or if it was the only establishment that would give us a job!'. Many of those appointed at this time settled in for a long stay and, if they moved on to promotion, did so with mixed feelings as John Sheppard recalls: 'as I stood on the steps under the tower and had a last look at the cricket being played on the field on a beautiful sunny day, the thought that came into my mind was "You bloody fool! What have you done?" Fortunately for me that next step proved to be a happy one but my debt to Moseley is still as vivid in my mind as it has ever been.'

Mr David Hebden, who has continued this tradition, remembers 'arriving in 1963 as a Sixth Form student, and returning in 1970 as a teacher, the most vivid impression was of a teaching staff which was virtually unchanged'. But more importantly 'they didn't patronise me as a former student, or treat me as anything other than their equal'. This impression is confirmed by Mr Pete Samuels who, having been offered his first teaching post at Moseley Modern in 1974, suddenly found himself in the same department as his former 'masters' when the schools amalgamated.

The life of a teacher must have been somewhat pleasanter than it is today, although Mr Malcolm Cook, who joined the staff in 1970 and stayed for 26 years, does remember that 'not all classes were easy; 30 frustrated adolescent males could be hard work for younger staff'. It remained an all-male institution, with the exception of Miss Marjorie Goode, the school secretary, until the problems of recruiting well-qualified science teachers led in 1971 to the appointment of the first woman to join the staff since the Second World War. Malcolm Cook recalls that new members of staff were often referred to by their surnames by the older staff. But 'teachers were trusted to do a professional job, without interference, and did so'.

The General Inspection report of 1962 had not been quite so kind, commenting that 'some Heads of Department might profitably be more positive in the conduct of their departments'. Of the staff in general, however, it found that 'very few reveal standards of performance below competence and about half are above average in quality as teachers', requiring only a 'greater leavening of scholarship and more daring enterprise'. The Inspectors commented on the Headmaster's 'sound and liberal measures for the boys' welfare and general culture' and concluded that 'at the time of the last report (in 1948) the general standard of work, despite good work in some subjects, was not considered to be fully satisfactory. Although some problems still remain, the school has made very considerable progress since that time'. In fact it went on to become one of the most successful schools in Birmingham by all the measures that are now used to judge schools, outperforming in work and sport its great rivals, the neighbouring schools of the King Edward Foundation.

The school had provided a rich variety of extra-curricular activities from its earliest days. Many of these grew and flourished as new staff were appointed with diverse interests and enthusiasms. The Field Club expanded and developed in scope, culminating in the acquisition and renovation in 1968 of the cottage near Abergavenny which continues to be well used and much valued by the present school population. There were frequent and increasingly adventurous foreign trips which usually managed to bring back all the boys they had left with. Clubs catered for everything from jazz to chemistry. One of the many new introductions was The Moseley Society which 'stimulated interest in local, national and international affairs' by the use of visiting speakers and debates. Despite this 'stimulating' atmosphere the two current members of staff who had joined the Sixth Form as students recall, respectively, 'only being used to soccer

Work on the school cottage in the early days.

The cottage today

and having my football shirt ripped off my back in my first taste of sixth form games and Barrie Corless' rugby' and 'the Head's three blonde daughters'.

The philosophy behind all the extra-curricular activities, as articulated by Mr Gaskin, was that 'boredom and a sense of failure are fertile grounds for youthful idleness and wrongdoing' and, in keeping with the general approach, 'the emphasis is always more on achieving a reasonable degree of competence and enjoyment for the many than on fostering a high standard of attainment for the few'. One or two activities began to lose their appeal; the Combined Cadet Force was disbanded in the early 1960s, a sign of changing times, reflected in the publication in The Moseleian of anti-war poetry and articles on the Campaign for Nuclear Disarmament. But in most respects the pattern was one of increasing opportunities.

Despite the limitations of the tiny stage, an impressive sequence of productions was mounted. Enthusiasm was such that a triple bill of short plays was presented every Christmas followed by a major play later in the year, although it is not clear which production necessitated the expenditure on throat lozenges shown in this account from 1967:

> Ring 4/-
>
> Make up 15/-
>
> Liquid Paraffin 12/6
>
> Paper Handkerchiefs 7/6
>
> Strepsils 4/6

There were many outstanding performances and productions; in 1964 an extraordinary 'Merchant of Venice' held the audience spellbound, followed two years later by a magical version of 'The Bespoke Overcoat'. Doubts about the wisdom of attempting 'Hamlet' as a school play were triumphantly dispelled in 1969 as Anton Lesser gave a performance which is still remembered as the precursor to a distinguished professional career. Music too was beginning to involve large numbers of pupils and some very successful concerts were given. As always with Moseley, many tastes were catered for and individual achievements ranged from Robert Penkett reaching the final of the National Piano Concerto Competition in 1971 to Bev Bevan's contribution to the international reputation of the Electric Light Orchestra.

Anton Lesser as Hamlet

In sport Moseley held its place as one of the dominant schools in Birmingham. Rugby and athletics brought the early successes – and some intense rivalry with other strong sporting schools from across the Midlands.

Sports Day continued to be a major highlight of the Summer Term. The experience of finishing races up the 'killer' rise from the playground proved invaluable in inter-school competition!

The highlight of the rugby season was often the Reddings Sevens and the school frequently provided members of the Greater Birmingham side, with Don Lane being selected for England. Athletics exemplified the Moseley approach. The school won the Kenrick Shield a remarkable 11 times but usually had few outright winners; the points came from second and third places and from

The outstanding athletics team of 1957, which won the Kenrick Shield by a margin of 38 points – the fourth win in succession and one of many throughout the history of the event.

winning the relays. The outstanding athlete was Dave Noble who competed in the Decathlon at national level but died tragically at the age of 28.

Cricket had been less successful until the arrival of John Sheppard in 1956 resulted in a steady improvement with some very successful seasons and a number of boys achieving representative honours. Cross-country produced impressive results, with the school always well placed in the League and one remarkable season when Andy White won seven of the nine Division One races. In all these sports there were teams in every age group, as well as in swimming and gymnastics.

There was great support from staff, parents and boys. Mr Gaskin attended almost every event, out of a mixture of commitment and genuine enthusiasm. Living in the school, his family became involved in everything that went on, his daughters acquiring an in-depth knowledge of the finer points of rugby, cricket and athletics which has proved invaluable. A complete cross-section of staff gave up their time to manage teams. Mr Charles Stewart, who had succeeded throughout his previous teaching career in avoiding all contact with team games, found himself soon after his arrival cutting up oranges on Saturday morning! Newer introductions such as basketball, hockey, tennis and table-tennis quickly developed to a high standard, the latter team becoming National

A memorable rugby season in which the 1st XV lost only one match, scored 258 points and conceded only 57. Many of the team played for Greater Birmingham and D.J. Garrett was appointed captain.

Schools Champions in 1969. The results of the tiddley-winks team which was founded in that same year and played all its matches against girls' schools were less remarkable.

In 1962 the decision was taken to build a sports pavilion in partnership with the Local Education Authority which gave the project its blessing – but not much else! Various fundraising committees began work; these were the days of summer fetes, bring and buy sales, raffles, car-washing and silver paper collections. The Parents' Committee, chaired by Mrs Gaskin, comprised an incredibly loyal nucleus of members who committed hours of their time and large sums of their own money to make each event a success. Despite constant

Members of the Parents' Committee at a fundraising meeting in the Head's garden in 1963. Mr and Mrs Gaskin are on the right.

setbacks and rising costs, the project kept going somehow. A group of parents offered to provide most of the materials and transport, and teams of boys led by Head of PE Mr John Reid and other members of staff undertook much of the building work. The pavilion was eventually opened in December 1965 with the heartfelt words 'Had anyone realised what was involved, the project might never have been started'. Recently extended and completely refurbished, it is still in constant use.

The 'magnificent but crumbling buildings' described by Malcolm Cook on his arrival had been causing problems for a number of years. Soon after Mr Gaskin's arrival it was found that the joists and floorboards in the headmaster's house were riddled with dry rot and all that had prevented the family from falling fifteen feet into the stone cellar below was a layer of linoleum. While the repair work was going on, the only way of reaching the bedrooms was through the main school corridor!

Despite the addition of a block housing art and dining rooms and the creation of a new playground, there was a serious shortage of space. The biggest problem seems to have been the lack of well-equipped laboratories for science, if Mr Hingley's frequent memos to the Head are anything to go by! By the mid-sixties

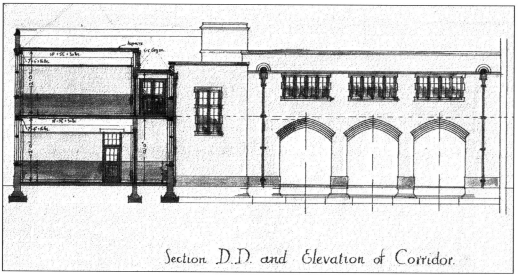

Section *D.D.* and Elevation of Corridor.

The 1920s extension, originally the science laboratories, was a well-proportioned building, sympathetically linked to the original building. Pressure of space in the 1950s and 60s led to further additions which destroyed the lines of the extension.

it had been agreed that new laboratories were urgently needed and work began on the block adjacent to the west wing. Surprise has been expressed on many occasions since at the siting of this extension (which was not originally joined to the main building) but it is clear with hindsight that a long-term decision had already been taken that the Victorian wings would at some stage be demolished and the Science block would form the first phase of the new building.

The building in winter in the late 1960s showing the first phase of the new Science block on the left.

The impressions articulated by David Hebden were probably shared by most pupils and many staff:

> *The effect of being educated in a building of such architectural worth, with its own rich and varied history, made less impact at the time than the inconveniences of cramped and dingy rooms, inadequate and dangerous gymnasium and poor indoor sporting facilities. It was with hindsight that one could see the benefit of learning in this cloistered atmosphere...*

The General Inspection report, however, had only one criticism of the accommodation and that concerned the Prefects' Room of which 'it is to be hoped that in time it will be more tastefully furnished'. Despite the problems it caused in the efficient running of the school, the building has always contributed significantly to the atmosphere of Moseley and in 1972 a successful application was made for it to be listed as a 'building of Special Architectural or Historical Interest'.

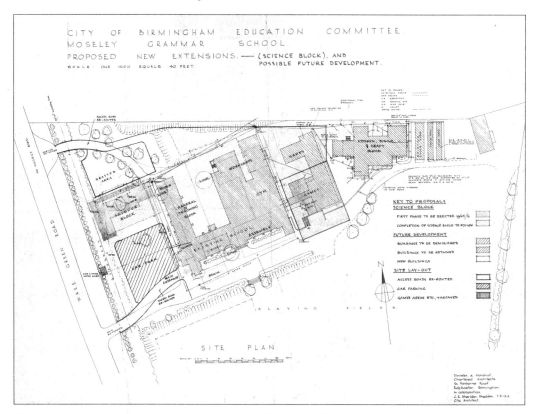

This plan shows quite clearly that the possibility of demolishing the Victorian building was being discussed by the City Council as early as 1963 when this was drawn up. At that stage no serious problems with the building had yet been found.

The school's surroundings were changing fast. In the late 1950s the last remaining section of the Moseley Botanical Gardens between the school and College Road was sold for building. Known as the 'Dell', it was a favourite shortcut for boys on their way home and still contained some fascinating relics of the Victorian pleasure garden it had once been. As it disappeared under the bricks and mortar of Pickwick Grove, the school itself only narrowly escaped demolition. A small boy using the shortcut home for lunch found some interesting looking objects left outside the workmen's hut and put them in his pocket. Within the hour the builders had notified the police that several sticks of gelignite, rejected because they had become unstable, had been stolen from the site.

The school fell under suspicion and a whole-school assembly was immediately called. Mr Gaskin explained to a hushed hall that the material was extremely dangerous, could detonate at any moment and should not under any circumstances be touched. Whereupon, a small hand started waving something in the air and a voice said 'Sir! Sir! It's alright, Sir! It's here, Sir!'. Mr Gaskin walked slowly towards the speaker, took the sticks of gelignite and kept walking until

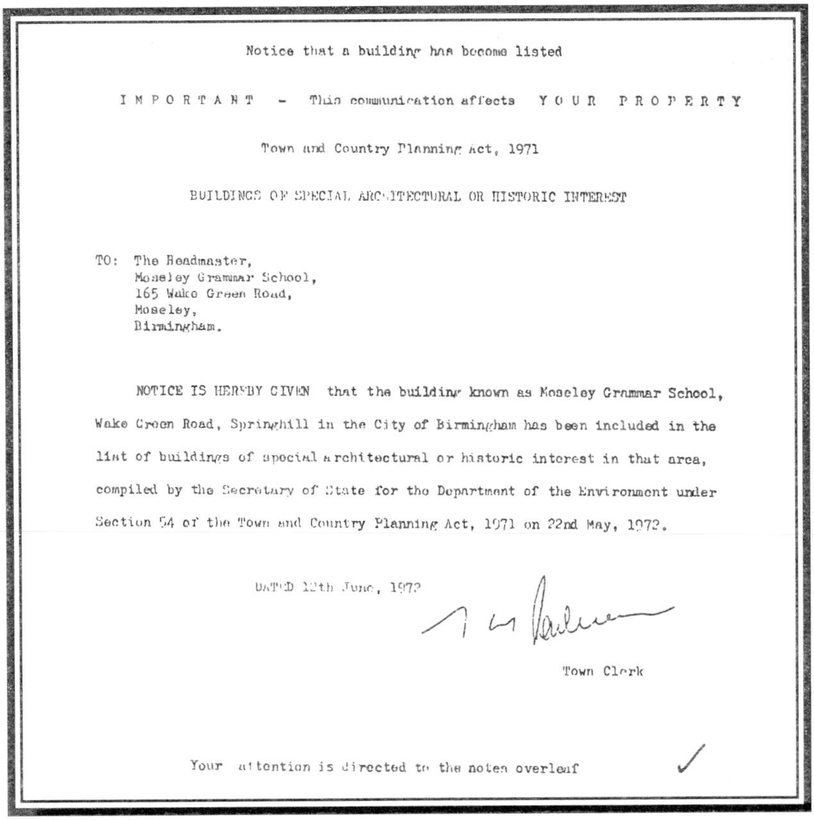

Notice that a building has become listed

IMPORTANT - This communication affects YOUR PROPERTY

Town and Country Planning Act, 1971

BUILDINGS OF SPECIAL ARCHITECTURAL OR HISTORIC INTEREST

TO: The Headmaster,
Moseley Grammar School,
165 Wake Green Road,
Moseley,
Birmingham.

NOTICE IS HEREBY GIVEN that the building known as Moseley Grammar School, Wake Green Road, Springhill in the City of Birmingham has been included in the list of buildings of special architectural or historic interest in that area, compiled by the Secretary of State for the Department of the Environment under Section 54 of the Town and Country Planning Act, 1971 on 22nd May, 1972.

DATED 12th June, 1972

Town Clerk

Your attention is directed to the notes overleaf

The letter confirming the building's Listed status –
a rather unimpressive document for something that was to prove so important.

he was well away from the building. What he said has unfortunately not been recorded. This episode will be familiar to admirers of Jasper Carrott who was a Second Form pupil at the time and who tells a rather more dramatic version of it!

Old Moseleians have distinguished themselves in almost every aspect of life and the school has enjoyed very close relations with the Moseleians for much of its existence. It was a mutually beneficial relationship with the Moseleians providing prizes and encouragement and the school providing new members for the very successful cricket and rugby teams. While the teams played their matches on Windermere Road Playing Fields, they were well supported by spectators from the school, but in 1961 they acquired the lease on land at Lugtrout Lane in Solihull and set about building a clubhouse. This was opened the following year and new members from school were strongly encouraged to swell the numbers and ensure the success of the venture.

However, the problems were already beginning to show. The dramatic expansion of Higher Education in the sixties meant more and more school-leavers moving away from Birmingham into universities and colleges around the country. Records of those who left in 1961 show that 58 went to university and 31 to various colleges; those who remained found Lugtrout Lane inaccessible without a car and these two factors must have contributed to the 1968 decision to change to an 'open' club, as the teams had already done. Financial pressures caused by the expenditure on the site led to a great emphasis on the importance of bar takings. Mr Gaskin felt that school-leavers and current pupils were being encouraged to drink unwisely and that some inappropriate entertainments were taking place. He severed the official link between the school and the Old Moseleians but remained on close and friendly terms with many individual members.

The first plans for the reorganisation of the city's schools along comprehensive lines appeared in the 1960s and it was obvious that the amalgamation of the two Moseley schools would feature in the plans. Mr Gaskin had been dissatisfied with the 11-plus for many years and was, unusually for a grammar school Head, a strong supporter of comprehensive schools. This view came to be shared by many Moseley Grammar School staff. There was also a perception that Moseley Modern was a very successful school and that there was little to fear from amalgamation. Obviously not all staff shared this view and Mr Gaskin worked hard to prepare the ground for a successful amalgamation. As the plans went backwards and forwards, however, it was clear that time was running out and that he would be close to retiring age when the change finally took place. He felt that his successor should be in position in good time to make the key decisions. This did not in the event happen, but it was clear that he was leaving the school in very good shape and in the very capable hands of his former deputy, Mr Derek Moore.

In his final Speech Day address, Mr Gaskin summed up his lifetime in teaching as 'an intensely rewarding experience, not in the financial sense, God knows, but in the human one'. This aspect of his leadership comes up frequently in the assessments of others. He believed unshakeably that every pupil in a school 'is of equal importance and entitled to an equal share of our attention' and he carried this attitude into his dealings with colleagues too. He was a man of considerable learning who made a significant contribution to educational thinking through his work on many advisory bodies and, after his retirement, as a governor of both Yardleys and Moseley Schools. He treated everyone he dealt with from the Chief Education Officer downwards with great courtesy but as his equal, as the informality of this brief note to the HMI leading the General Inspection team shows:

> *The remaining forms should be sent off tomorrow; the other documents you require, with luck, early next week.*
>
> *In haste,*
>
> *D.B.G.*

David Hebden observes that Mr Gaskin:

> *...commanded great respect for his own learning, his complete mastery of his job and his ability to deal well with people. He conveyed to his teachers his respect for their abilities. They were certainly afraid of him in the sense that they held him in awe. Yet before entering the Staff Common Room, he would always knock.*

He genuinely admired the talents of others; he would have loved to paint like Lou Emery, direct plays like Bert Briscoe, conduct Belshazzar's Feast like David Sadler and place-kick like Ron Walker! But his control of the school was total. Malcolm Cook calls him a 'magisterial headmaster ... with natural authority' but also recalls 'his wicked sense of humour'.

This, along with his 'intellectual eminence, dedication and high principles', are remembered by Derek Moore, who also pays tribute to Mrs Gaskin:

> *We always recognised her charm and her deep and real interest in the school. Perhaps her greatest strength was that she, recognising her husband's singular qualities for so important a task, shared and encouraged him in his devotion to education in general, Moseley Grammar School in particular.*

Mr Gaskin had complete confidence that Moseley would always be a fine school. Derek Moore refers to 'his joyous optimism' and his belief 'that education is possibly the most powerful force for good'. He had presided over a splendid era in the school's history but he concluded his last address looking forward not back, with the words:

> *I am not one of those who indulge in emotive talk about schools being destroyed. Nothing can destroy what this school has achieved in the last fifty years ... If our present structure is to change, I do not doubt that this record will be an inspiration ... In the end, whether a school is large or small, mixed or single-sex, primary or secondary, selective, non-selective or comprehensive, everything comes back to the capacities and the attitudes of those who compose it and those who run it.*

References and acknowledgements

Once again we are indebted to Roy Holloway for cataloguing the complete set of The Moseleian magazines for this period. Additional information and newspaper articles are held by the Birmingham Central Library, and files by Moseley School. Our thanks to Betty Gaskin, John Sheppard, David Hebden, Malcolm Cook, Graham Bate, Pete Samuels and Derek Moore for their recollections; to Dave Clements for the loan of photographs and to Birmingham Design Services for the loan of architects' drawings.

Chapter Seven

The Amalgamation of the two Moseley Schools 1972-1974

The process of moving to a system of comprehensive schools was as bitterly fought in Birmingham as anywhere in the country and led to a period of great uncertainty for all the schools involved. From the first publication of proposals in the 1960s to the final amalgamation in September 1974 the plans went backwards and forwards between the Education Committee and the Secretary of State as control of the City Council changed hands and various vested interests in the city tried to influence events.

The first plans were drawn up by the then Chief Education Officer Sir Lionel Russell as a result of the Circular sent out by the Labour Government in 1965, inviting Local Education Authorities to submit within a year plans for reorganising secondary education along comprehensive lines. The proposals endorsed by the Labour Education Committee Chairman, Councillor Nigel Cook, were based on 11-18 mainly mixed comprehensives and envisaged the two Moseley schools combining to provide a 1,470 possibly boys' comprehensive – presumably to match the 1,290 places for girls at the combined Swanshurst schools. Only the maintained schools were involved; there were no proposals to involve the King Edward Foundation schools but 'talks were to be held...'. Many other aspects of this original plan were later dropped; it was put forward 'as a basis for discussion', the tone of which was set by the Conservative spokesman, Alderman Sydney Dawes, who spoke of the 'Socialists so obsessed with furthering the cause of comprehensive education' and of parents being 'violently opposed' to the idea.

By the summer of 1970 the Conservatives had taken control of the Council and Alderman Dawes began drawing up a series of proposals with a very different agenda. Mrs Thatcher was now Secretary of State for Education and immediately withdrew the 1965 Circular. Those in favour of comprehensive schools realised belatedly that they had a fight on their hands and began to get organised, although they always had an uphill struggle. Moseley Grammar School made headlines when 30 of the 39 staff, including the Head and Deputy Head signed a city-wide petition calling for an end to the 11-plus. Mr Gaskin gave a lengthy interview to The Evening Mail in which he described Moseley as a fine school but said he was not happy 'while there are youngsters who are not getting the chance they deserve'. On educational grounds, he said, 'the case for a comprehensive system is overwhelming'.

Alderman Dawes produced three plans in all, of which the first two were rejected by his own side as they proposed a drastic reduction in selective places on the grounds that 'there are pupils in some schools who should not be there and cannot take advantage of the special academic demands of the grammar school'. The final version still meant a reduction in selective places, to be achieved by taking three less successful grammar schools out of the system and removing the small selective intake from the city's few pioneering comprehensives which were also to lose their designation and be known simply as 'schools', thus reducing them to the status of very large secondary modern schools. The pressure on selective accommodation would be reduced by raising the age of transfer from 11 to 12 years. The city's selective entry would be cut from 27 per cent to 16 per cent but the report claimed no-one would suffer because 'The aim would be to establish the same staffing ratios for all pupils up to the age of 16 and ... ensure that there will no longer be any grounds for the difference in public esteem which has hampered the best efforts of non-selective schools in the past'. This was greeted with derision by most of those working in the education service.

While teachers and their organisations led opposition to the plan the Conservatives lost control of the Council again. The Labour majority quickly put through a motion to abolish selection and in the summer of 1972 the new Chairman of the Education Committee, Councillor Miss Sheila Wright, began a series of public meetings with parents and teachers' groups to find out what kind of system they wanted. From this consultation process came the idea of organising consortium groupings based on districts and comprising between eight and ten secondary schools, some of which would be combined to form new comprehensives. All the consortium schools would work closely to provide a common curriculum up to the age of 16 and thereafter to pool resources for the benefit of sixth form students. The King Edward Foundation refused to take part in the consultation, although most of their schools were by now largely funded by the local authority.

A curious situation developed as the schools in each consortium worked quietly and constructively to develop this system, while all around them an increasingly acrimonious political dispute was going on. Opposition to the plan centred on the fact that the Education Committee had to publish individual notices under Section 13 of the 1944 Education Act for each school whose status they wished to change. The process could be delayed if ten electors objected to changes in each of the 98 schools involved. A campaign calling itself 'Save Our Schools' was launched in the autumn. It organised a public meeting and sent out forms for the registering of objections. Schools were immediately advised by the new Chief Education Officer Mr Kenneth Brooksbank not to send these out via pupils as 'the practice of the Education Committee has been to avoid using children in controversial issues'. The campaign should of course have been called 'Save our Grammar Schools'; there was no corresponding organisation trying to save the secondary moderns!

"Save Our Schools" Campaign

Director:
Mr. M. St. G. ARROWSMITH, M.A.
82, HAGLEY ROAD
EDGBASTON, BIRMINGHAM, B16 8LZ

Treasurer:
Mrs. J. M. YULE
33, GREENHILL ROAD
BIRMINGHAM, B13 9SS

The Headmaster and Chairman
of The Parent Teachers Association   12th October, 1972.

Now that the L.E.A. is about to publish Section 13 notices in respect of many Birmingham Secondary Schools we wish it to be known to EVERY school in Birmingham that this organisation is prepared and willing to assist any person or group of persons who wish to lodge an objection in respect of any school affected by the proposed scheme for the re-organisation of Secondary Education in Birmingham. We assume it is generally known that one cannot lodge a formal objection against the scheme as such.

We also wish all parents and members of the teaching professions in Birmingham to know that we are staging a rally at the Digbeth Institute on Tuesday, 24th October at 7.30 p.m. The rally will be addressed by local speakers well qualified to comment on the scheme and by Mr. Maynard Potts, M.A., M.Sc., Hon. F.R.I.B.A., Chairman of the National Education Association. This will be one of the very few meetings in Birmingham at which well informed platform speakers will have been encouraged to put forward constructive criticisms of the scheme and to give advice on how best to resist it.

Anyone wishing to attend the rally should apply for a ticket at the above address or from any S.O.S. Area Chairman. There will be no charge for admission but we wish to have an indication of the number likely to attend so that we may make adequate preparations. There will be limited provision for non-ticket holders but a ticket will ensure admission.

If you have a Parents Association at your school would you be so kind as to pass the enclosed copy of this letter to the Chairman. If you do not have a Parents Association we hope you will feel it incumbent upon you, in persuance of true democratic principles, to bring the letter to the attention of parents of children attending your school and to your staff in some other suitable manner.

Further information or advice will gladly be given on request to any individual who cares to seek it.

Yours sincerely,

Part of the 'Save our Schools' campaign

At the end of October, having already announced his retirement, Mr Gaskin held two very informal meetings for parents. Describing the public meetings which had taken place as 'dogfights between those who have already made up their minds' he outlined the plans in some detail. He reassured parents that the problems of size could be managed by good organisation, that the existing pupil entitlement would continue but with a wider choice of subjects, that the staff had some reservations but were determined to make it work and that *they* might be worried about mixed classes but their sons were not! He criticised Heads and teachers in other schools who were predicting disaster by warning that 'You can't cry stinking fish and then expect to sell it'.

Thus in January 1973 Mr Derek Moore took over as Acting Head to prepare the grammar school for amalgamation. He was as committed to the ideal as his predecessor and was supported by many on the staff, a group of whom, led by Mr Roy Pinney, submitted a paper actively welcoming the scheme but asking 'Will the Education Committee agree not to administer a selection examination for any schools next year, including those of The King Edward Foundation, even if they stay out of the scheme?' No answer has been traced. The Consortium Heads were now meeting more or less weekly, as were groups of teachers within the schools, and this continued throughout the spring and early summer.

The Education Committee, however, were aware that the Secretary of State Mrs Thatcher could reject enough of the plan to make it unworkable and made contingency arrangements. On 11 July she duly rejected the scheme and everything was put on hold for another year. But the staff continued meeting and planning, Derek Moore found himself expected to continue as Acting Head for three more terms and the life of the schools went on. In November the Chief Education Officer and the Education Committee Chairman came to explain to staff and parents that the scheme was being re-submitted and detailed planning should begin. Working parties were set up which identified·three priorities for the new school. These were:

- discipline: with a strong system of Year Heads and bases to offset the increased size

- academic achievement: to build on existing high standards

- a caring community: to blend the two schools together

Clear standards were laid down for pupils and teachers, together with strategies and sanctions for dealing with behaviour problems. The structure of the day, the organisation of pupils into groups and the new uniform were all agreed. It was necessary to plan around the constraints of existing staffing and accommodation as well as the commitment that pupils already in school could continue their courses unchanged. The most significant decision concerned the arrangement of teaching groups: it was decided to create three broad ability bands with mixed ability classes within each band. Timetabling was made very difficult by uncertainty about the new intake.

Finally at the end of May 1974, the amalgamation proposals were approved and in an extraordinary few weeks the new school was prepared for September. The main concern for the staff was the allocation of posts as there were two candidates for every vacancy. One member of the Modern School staff devised a board game called 'Grovel' which was similar to Monopoly and involved trying to circle the board performing various tasks in order to get a job! Some urgent alterations began, in particular the much discussed requirements for 'toilets for the girls and lady teachers' in the grammar school building.

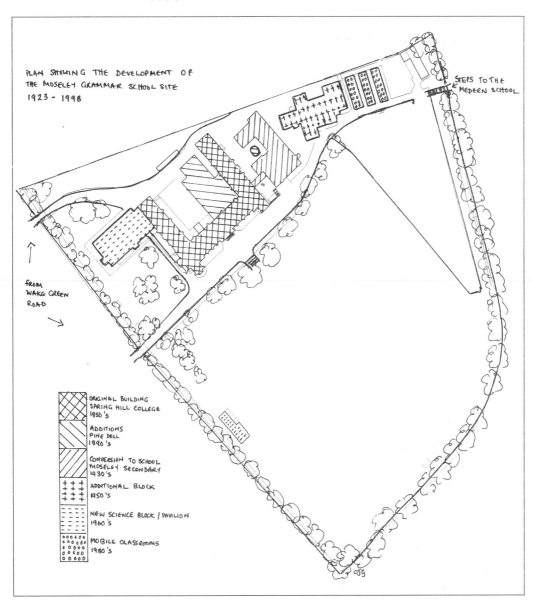

PLAN SHOWING THE DEVELOPMENT OF
THE MOSELEY GRAMMAR SCHOOL SITE
1923 - 1998

STEPS TO THE
MODERN SCHOOL

FROM
WAKE GREEN
ROAD

ORIGINAL BUILDING
SPRING HILL COLLEGE
1850's

ADDITIONS
PINE DELL
1890's

CONVERSION TO SCHOOL
MOSELEY SECONDARY
1930's

ADDITIONAL BLOCK
1950's

NEW SCIENCE BLOCK / PAVILION
1960's

MOBILE CLASSROOMS
1980's

It is hoped that the mobile classrooms will soon go and that the 1960s science block will eventually be rebuilt elsewhere on the site, thus restoring the original facade of the west wing.

Both staffs confidently expected 'their' Head to be appointed to run the new school. The interviews for all the new Headships took place, two a day, in the second week of July and, by a strange process not unlike musical chairs, the Head of Central Grammar School was appointed to run Moseley, the Head of Moseley Modern School was appointed to run Yardleys and the Acting Head of Moseley Grammar School was appointed to run Central Byng Kenrick. Mr

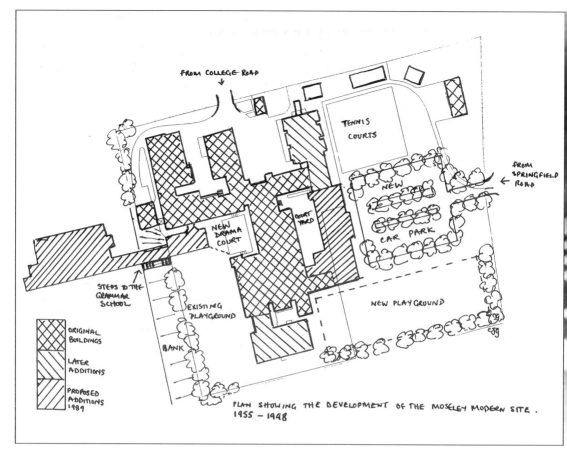

The proposed additions shown here will not now be needed. They were intended to provide the necessary extra space when the former Moseley Grammar School building was either knocked down or allowed to fall down.

Lockwood was confirmed as Moseley's Deputy Head, having been interviewed on the same day for three different Deputy Headships in three different rooms at the Education Office.

Thus Moseley School, where the majority of staff were in favour of amalgamation, prepared to welcome as Head Mr Alan Goodfellow, who had gone on record as saying that he was 'bitterly opposed' to the reorganisation. Mr Wilford and Mr Moore were both asked to take on schools where their grammar school predecessor and many of his staff had strongly opposed the plans. They left with deep reluctance, having committed themselves so much to the success of Moseley. Mr Wilford had confidently expected to get the job, a feeling reinforced by the expectations of his colleagues. His disappointment was compounded by the fact that Mr Goodfellow, on being offered the Moseley job, asked if he could defer his decision until after the Central Byng Kenrick interviews. His request was turned down and he therefore accepted the Moseley job with visible reluctance. Mr Moore was less upset, having expected less, but still describes his 14 years at Moseley as 'a period of joy'.

These upheavals caused some resentment at the time, but there was little opportunity to dwell on it. All three new Heads spent August clearing up at their previous schools and preparing for the start of term in their new schools at the beginning of September. In the end, the amalgamation of the two Moseley Schools was less traumatic than similar changes across the city. Although there were doubts on both sides about the size of the new school and the suddenness of the change, both staffs knew it was going forward with much goodwill on both sides. Pupils and parents could see that it was going to offer a wide range of opportunities. It was viewed in the city as the merger of two already fine schools and expectations of what it could achieve were high.

References and acknowledgements

This chapter relies mainly on the records held by the Birmingham Central Library and on newspaper articles of the time. We have also had access to the School's files and to Mr Gaskin's personal records and speeches. Our thanks to Derek Moore, John Lockwood, Brian Miles, Steve Rosson and Betty Gillespie for their help.

Chapter Eight

Moseley School 1974-1998

Between the end of May and the beginning of September 1974, Moseley School came into being. After all the delays of the preceding years, in the end the pace of change was dramatic. The broad outlines of policy were in place and some detail had been worked out but Mr John Lockwood had from June to August to devise a timetable for the new school and Mr Goodfellow had even less time to decide on the key appointments. Mrs Betty Gillespie remembers:

> *In the September, the only thing done by the Authority towards the amalgamation was the building of the steps between the two sites. At that stage nothing was done to provide toilet facilities for any girls using the West Wing. Initially the two schools had a different school day. The Grammar School had always had five lessons in the morning, and three in the afternoon, while the Mixed School had four morning and four afternoon. Starting and finishing times, and lunch times, were not the same either so that the school day was obviously one of the first changes to be made.*

Despite Mr Goodfellow's initial reluctance to take the job, understandable since he was well established at Central, he is generally considered to have done an excellent job. Responsibilities and routines were quickly in place; many of those involved refer to a 'smooth transition'.

It was of course a gradual change. Only the new intake of pupils was fully integrated. Many staff continued with an almost unchanged teaching load. The problem of posts of responsibility was mainly solved by appointing the grammar school staff to Head of Department posts and the modern school staff to pastoral posts such as Heads of Year. The exceptions were at Deputy Head level where Mr John Lockwood took the academic area of responsibility and Mr Philip Bullock took the pastoral side. Depending on who you talk to, this was either considered 'a fair and sensible arrangement' or was 'much resented'. There is, however, no difference of opinion concerning Mr Goodfellow's ability to make decisions and solve problems. He 'quickly earned respect' by tackling some contentious issues head on. For example, he confronted the apprehensions of some of the grammar school staff about having to work with women (although it was not the first time) – and teach girls – by moving two traditionally female departments into the grammar school building, now known as West Wing. One of these was Betty Gillespie's:

> *Mr Goodfellow felt it was appropriate for some girls to be based in West Wing on a permanent basis, and as the Business Studies Department was mostly girls at that time we moved yet again, into two rooms on the first floor leading to the new Science Block, overlooking the Headmaster's garden. The Physics Department cleared out the third room on that corridor which they were using for storage, and we then had our usual three adjacent rooms. This move was not too popular with some members of the previous Grammar School staff and some of their comments in the Staff Room, which were passed on to me, were not exactly welcoming!*

It was not only the grammar school staff who needed to change in this respect. Despite having been a mixed school from the outset, there was a strong perception among experienced women staff at the modern school of a rather 'laddish' culture with an emphasis on male bonding through sport and practical jokes.

Such a perception of course depends on your point of view. To Mr Steve Rosson it was quite different: 'As a young man I found the staff sports fixtures a marvellous force for coherence as we socialised with people from all different departments and from both sets of staff'. He recalls another factor which brought the staff together: 'No-one had a set room to teach in and, whilst this had its disadvantages, it had the major advantage of making staff move around, get familiar with both buildings and meet other teachers'. This was clearly an important concern. Mr Malcolm Cook remembers 'there was little mixing of the two staffs initially, partly because of the separate "wings" and partly because the personnel were so different'.

He was, however, in the forefront. 'Being relatively new, I led the first Moseley Grammar School class down the hill, across the fence to a very fine classroom in the East Wing, a neat file of rather resentful Year Nine boys in smart black uniforms.' Those travelling the other way were less impressed. Betty Gillespie's recollections of West Wing are of 'Dickensian conditions in the staffroom' and:

> *...a beautiful old building which had suffered a great deal of neglect! Wall plaster was crumbling in many places, some windows were stuffed up with newspapers to stop the draughts and others were so ill-fitting due to crumbling outside masonry that the wind whistled in and at times could blow papers off the desk! Some window frames had been painted over so many times that they wouldn't open, others wouldn't shut properly as the catches were broken, and the whole place really looked shabby and in need of some 'tender loving care' – it seemed such a shame, in what was basically a lovely building.*

On a more positive note, she recalls:

> *The girls certainly appreciated the old building and welcomed the move. They thought it was very quaint to have stone angels in the corners of some of the rooms downstairs, and liked to stand at the end and look down the length of the bottom corridor which appeared like a cloister – shades of the original Theological College! They were full of praise for the Library, although they originally found the selection of books very different from those available in the Mixed School. We all appreciated the fact that the whole building had a quieter atmosphere than the East Wing and felt this was more conducive to serious endeavour.*

On the whole the modern school staff had a more upbeat attitude to the new situation. They felt they had more to gain, they were used to dealing with girls and 'problem' pupils and they were also used to a much greater degree of staff mobility than their grammar school counterparts; they had experience of moving school and of mixing with new colleagues, while many of the grammar school staff had spent their entire careers in the same school and with the same people. Few of the latter attended the 'Amalgamation Dance' and those who did were 'astonished by the informality, bordering on the anarchic, with staff such as Mr Lockwood (Deputy Head) dressing up!' as Malcolm Cook recalls, adding 'we enjoyed it'. The modern school staff certainly introduced a note of irreverence as when 'Mr Goodfellow stressed that Heads of Department and Heads of Year were in effect Company Executives and should work and behave as such. Several immediately applied for company cars!' according to Mr Brian Miles.

But the key elements which ensured the 'smooth start' which Moseley enjoyed and many amalgamated schools did not were the wise and even-handed leadership provided by Mr Goodfellow and the mutual respect and tolerance shown by the two staffs. Mr David Hebden describes how 'it was refreshing to see how attitudes changed...new alliances formed, ability in new colleagues grudgingly – at first – recognised, and inadequacies among former colleagues gradually admitted'. Steve Rosson talks of both groups of staff showing 'tolerance and understanding of each other' and, almost with an air of surprise, of 'many grammar school teachers who genuinely supported the comprehensive ideal'. A musical entitled 'West Wing Story', loosely based on 'West Side Story' and featuring the romance between a grammar and a secondary modern teacher, was performed by staff for staff at an early social function and certainly helped to break the ice!

Contact between the two sets of pupils was not always quite so civilised. There was inevitably some sorting out of the pecking order in the less visible corners of the site at breaks and lunchtimes. The longstanding rivalry between the Modern School's soccer teams and the Grammar School's rugby teams

Successful productions continued, such as Beauty and the Beast in 1976, written by drama teacher, Mr Harry Nash and starring Mr Pete Samuels – heavily disguised!

More immediately recognisable to today's pupils would be Mrs Angela Billingham (standing) who was involved in many productions at this time.

was finally settled when the PE staff organised a match between them. It would be interesting to know what rules they played by! Both sports, however, continued to enjoy success for some years. The rugby teams produced at least one outstanding player in Eddie Saunders, who was capped by the Barbarians; they also took part in a legendary tour of which stories abound!

There were pleasant surprises on both sides. Malcolm Cook describes being 'less traumatised by "the less academic" pupils than many mainly older staff' and found 'having girls in classes a very civilising influence'. Perhaps most importantly, 'academic standards held up remarkably well. In my own subject A Level results actually improved with a pass rate of between 80 per cent and 95 per cent.' It was an exciting time to be a pupil at Moseley, as many have confirmed. There was a huge range of activities on offer with the combined talents of the two staffs in drama and music, with a wider choice of sports and access to the school cottage extended to a whole new group of enthusiasts. It was a 'happy, well-balanced and successful place, despite its size'.

Mr Goodfellow's time at Moseley was, however, to be dogged by ill-health. He suffered a series of heart attacks and during his absences first Mr Philip Bullock and then John Lockwood took over as Acting Heads. But the school continued to flourish. It had retained most of its well-qualified and experienced staff and enjoyed a genuinely 'comprehensive' intake with a good balance of pupils from all the surrounding areas. Many of them remember the school with affection even if they experienced some turbulent times.

The school cottage began to receive parties of girls for the first time.

Becky Hopkins (nee Wyatt) remembers 'Mr Brown was terrible. In our form diary he wrote "Rebecca should think about wearing a longer skirt". In the next lesson I decided to have this out with him and the class would back me up. They didn't.' The most useful part of her education was perhaps not quite what the school intended: 'Moseley equipped me with confidence. I developed good problem solving skills sitting in the toilets in West Wing and hearing people's problems because they thought I was worldly wise'. But overall 'It was a good school. I regret not working harder and wish I'd knuckled down ... I did what was right for me at the time ... I enjoyed my schooldays'.

There was much to enjoy. The school cottage was being constantly improved and extended, supported by fund-raising activities like the sponsored walk in 1981 from school to the cottage, a distance of 100 miles. Led by Mr John Webb, 25 walkers and a dog were seen off by Warwickshire cricketer and former pupil Steve Rouse. Brian Miles led the back up crew who pitched tents and cooked for the group. The walk took four and a half days and raised over £1000 to build another dormitory. A similar event in 1984 involved four teams – two from the staff, one from the parents and one from the Sixth Form in a relay marathon over the same distance. Other groups since have cycled the route to raise money for charity.

Headteacher Mr David Swinfen in happier times, completing a staff half-marathon organised 'for fun' in 1985.

Mr Goodfellow died in 1982 and interviews were held to appoint a new Head. No appointment was made and the job was readvertised. This time the post was offered to one of the original applicants Mr David Swinfen. John Lockwood decided to retire at this point and Mrs Mary Miles was subsequently appointed as Deputy Head. Mr Swinfen set about changing some of the more traditional aspects of Moseley which had continued since amalgamation but events beyond his control were about to overwhelm the school.

The first of these followed the redrawing of the school's catchment area to exclude parts of Hall Green which had traditionally sent pupils to Moseley and to include a large area of Sparkbrook. Thus the school began receiving pupils from an area of Birmingham associated with deprivation, unemployment, poor housing and chronic ill-health. Their needs have put considerable extra demands on the school's resources. There is now a sophisticated network of support and a whole range of study facilities including participation in Birmingham's exciting University of the First Age.

More trouble was looming, this time dictated by national events. Just as Birmingham might have been forgiven for thinking that education was emerging from the political battleground of the reorganisation era into a period of relative calm, the entire state education system was about to be turned upside down by Mrs Thatcher's government. But Moseley had other problems closer to home. A battle to save its original Victorian building began in 1984, when the City Architect's Department was asked to carry out a feasibility study on the provision of improvements to the Sixth Form accommodation. Its report, submitted in May 1985, detailed remodelling, conversions and improvements and was 'received favourably' by the Education Department. To prepare for the structural improvements, further inspections of timbers in the Headmaster's House were made, with alarming results. Timbers were found to be 'rife with beetle infestation and dormant dry rot was also prevalent', as well as 'wet rot to the joist ends'.

Although this was not the first time problems had been identified – the severity of defects noticed by the school's occupants had warranted inspection by the City Engineer as early as July 1982 (and had been noted during the original conversion of the building in the 1920s) - the Council now pursued the matter. Specialist investigation of the Library revealed extensive damage by the True Dry Rot fungus (Serpula lacrymans) and wide-spread decay by the Wet Rot fungus (Coniophora puteana), as well as 'bowing out' of the front wall. The report recommended '*urgent* consideration be given to scaffolding the complete core of this area using a scaffold suitable for propping and supporting the complete roof'.

The 'potential danger of the possible collapse of the roof of the Library' led to the erection of 'an internal framed scaffolding dead-shore and external raking shores, to restrain the parapet displaced by the lateral thrust from the distorted trusses'. The actual closure of the library occurred in rather dramatic fashion. Mr Pete Anstey recalls that he was invigilating an A Level examination,

The life of the school went on around the closed off and heavily scaffolded library.

Internal scaffolding prevented the collapse of the hammer beam roof.

when the Head Mr Swinfen and two architects came in, announcing that the library was to be closed forthwith. After some discussion, the examination continued under Mr Swinfen's supervision, and only when papers were handed in was the closure order executed. It is not recorded what effect this historic interruption had on the performance of the students and their exam grades!

Plans for the Sixth Form area were suspended and gradually more and more areas of the old building were closed. The upper floors were shut off and finally the administration offices were relocated from the Headmaster's house, which was also closed. The City Architect's 1986 Investigation of the Building's Defects and Delapidation (sic) recommended that 'in order to avoid the total loss of the major part of this school, remedial works should be carried out to the whole of this area urgently and effectively'. Despite this, in the following four years nothing was done.

Further scaffolding was required when the roof of the tower was found to be on the point of collapse.

Meanwhile the Thatcher 'revolution' was gathering pace. Local Education Authorities and schools were identified as obstructing the overall aim of 'the elimination of socialism' as she told the Daily Mail in May 1987 and she promised 'a revolution in the running of the schools'. The 1988 Education Act was thus almost entirely political rather than educational in its intentions. It sought first to 'break' the (mainly Labour) local authorities by removing much of the funding and control of education, their largest area of responsibility.

Secondly the Act sought to create a competitive system with successful schools winning more funding and more pupils. Under the banner of 'freedom' and 'parental choice' this has actually created a hierarchy of schools remarkably similar to the era of the 11-plus. Thirdly it sought to control the curriculum in a way unprecedented in the history of English schools. The official justification for this, as propounded by its Tory instigators and adopted by their Labour successors, is that the comprehensive system is failing. Many educators consider this view to be based on political expediency not educational evidence; some would go so far as to say that it is a response to the very success of comprehensive schooling which has created aspirations among the young that the country cannot afford to match.

The effect of this wide-ranging Act on Moseley School has been considerable. The first provision described above limited the support the LEA could give as the school underwent its rapid and massive demographic change. The second had a more dramatic effect. As the council's changes to the catchment area brought increasing numbers of Asian children into Moseley School, the new system of open enrolment allowed white parents in the school's traditional catchment area to send their children over the border into Solihull, destabilising the balanced intake which had made the school so successful since amalgamation.

The third provision imposed on the school not one National Curriculum but successive versions requiring constant changes in planning and resourcing at a time when it was having to adapt at breakneck speed to the needs of its new intake. The publication of league tables based on the crude results of tests has also been damaging to the reputation of a school where the majority of pupils have English as a second language and whose dramatic progress is not shown. There is no way of recording the achievements of 12 year olds who escort their parents to Parents' Evenings and conduct lengthy discussions with their teachers about the demands of the National Curriculum while simultaneously translating into Punjabi or Urdu for their parents.

The school suffered other problems at this time. The steep flight of steps which had been cut through the bank to link the two buildings together proved disastrous during a violent thunderstorm. Water poured down the bank from West Wing, through the gap and across the playground into East Wing. As the water level rose, Pete Anstey built a barricade of blackboards to channel the flow through the building and at a given signal opened the front doors to let the river pour through and out into College Road. At its worst the water had been several feet deep; one lad dived in and swam across the canteen. Damage was considerable. All the ground floor offices were wrecked and everything was lost, including the entire records of Moseley Modern School. More spectacularly, the hall floor had lifted in a series of peaks and troughs and balanced on one of the peaks was the grand piano! Torrential rain produced the same results on at least two more occasions before the simple solution of building a barrier similar to a speed bump to turn the playground into a holding 'lake'.

The problems with the original Victorian building continued. Four years had passed 'without any remedial action being taken', according to the 1990 City Architect's report. The 'temporary scaffolding support structure has satisfactorily continued to achieve its purpose both internally and externally' but the West Wing remained unoccupied and locked, while water, rot fungus and pigeon colonies furthered the decay of the building. The inaction of the council was due to its espousal in 1987 of a different solution to the dilapidation of the school.

In September of that year, the city's Schools Sub-committee agreed to recommend that the school be demolished, rather than pay the £3.6 million it would cost to save it. This was against the recommendation of the Chief Education Officer and in spite of its Grade II listed status, granted in 1972. A representative opined that the council was in 'an impossible position': 'on the one hand we would be criticised for seeking to demolish part of Birmingham's Victorian heritage, while on the other hand we would be criticised for spending over £3 million on repairs to one school when we have scarcely more than that amount available for the whole year'.

We the undersigned, electors in the City of Birmingham, utterly reject and deplore the decision of the Education Schools' Sub-Committee to seek permission to demolish the historic part of Moseley School. We urge the City Council to seek ways to reinstate a unique building serving this highly successful and popular school.

NAME   **ADDRESS**   **SIGNATURE**

....

The petition launched in 1987 against the proposal to demolish West Wing which collected 18,000 signatures in a few days.

The reaction from the public was immediate. A campaign to save the Victorian building was launched by parents, governors, teachers and former students, 500 attended a protest meeting and a massive petition of over 18,000 signatures was collected in just a few days. An Action Committee was formed with teacher-governor Mr David Hebden as Chair, and including local historian Mr Maurice White, parent-governor Mr Ron Kinsler and the Chair of Governors Mr S. K. Basu, who called the decision 'tantamount to vandalism on a grand scale'. Distinguished old boys Jasper Carrott, Bev Bevan, Sir Alan Cottrell, former Master of Jesus College, Cambridge, and TV news reporter Anthony Carthew lent their support to the campaign.

The Birmingham Post and Evening Mail were deluged with letters of protest. They attacked the 'arrogance' of the council in being prepared 'to spend £9.5 million of ratepayers' money to build a new school instead of restoring the fine old building' and raised questions about the legality of levelling a Grade II listed building. Parent governor Mrs P. Holt expressed her 'total horror and dismay' at the decision and asked whether the members of the sub-committee had ever visited the school or 'even taken the trouble to consider the excellent standard of education provided by this multi-cultural comprehensive school'. A letter from former headmaster Mr D. B. Gaskin described as 'singularly inept and insensitive' Councillor Jim Eames' characterisation of the building as 'a pile of rubble holding itself together'. Mr Gaskin evoked 'the deep affection' of generations of former pupils for this 'remarkable Victorian architectural survival' and concluded that 'it would indeed be an act of inexcusable Philistinism to pull it down'.

The strength of feeling and the breadth of support were irresistible and, just two weeks after announcing its decision, the council backed down. The reversal was unexpected. David Hebden tells how the Action Committee attended a public meeting with the council, armed with evidence of the strength of the opposition, and prepared for a showdown. The council 'cut the ground from under our feet' and pre-empted the Committee's planned protest by announcing that the decision had been reversed. Instead, the council agreed to work with the Moseley School Action Committee to explore ways of raising the funds. They decided to employ a firm of professional fund-raisers, Donors' International, and made public statements about setting up a charitable trust to obtain cash backing from official government bodies, charities, conservation trusts, private donations and fundraising events.

But this did not happen, and subsequent events cast doubts on the good faith of certain participants in this process. Donors International met with the Action Committee regularly for a year, but appeared to have 'no ideas' and to show 'a lack of purpose and urgency'. Suspicions have since been voiced that the company was paid by the council to stall the process and that the council was merely 'playing for time'. At the end of the year, the Committee met with Donors International and presented criticisms of all their actions (or inactions), which the company refuted. A delegation from the Committee – the Chair, chair of governors and a parent-governor – then met with the council to complain about Donors International. By 1989, the council had paid off the professional fundraisers who, according to David Hebden, 'had failed to professionally fundraise one penny'.

The heat had gone out of the public campaign to save the building, and a further year or so of inaction followed. However in 1989, plans were drawn up by the council for a completely new school to be built on the East Wing site, the former Moseley Modern School. The plans show a range of options for cramming a new smaller school into the limited site, with considerable curtailment of playground space. They do not indicate what was to be the fate of the original Moseley School site, but it is widely assumed by those involved at the school that the intention was to let the Victorian building decay beyond repair and then sell the land for development.

The building plan, however, came to nothing. In 1990 the City Architect was asked to update the earlier report of the deterioration of the West Wing building. The report highlights the scale of the work needed to restore it to use, and paints a depressing picture: the parapet over the main entrance 'has obviously moved and is clearly leaning out', brickwork has deteriorated, rubbish is accumulating in lightwells, stairwells and on the roof, the 'pigeon aviary to the tower is obviously flourishing', wild growths of vegetation have increased rising damp problems, timber decay is obviously spreading, moisture penetration has worsened and deterioration of the plaster increased. The report concludes that 'it is without exaggeration that it can be expected for the deterioration to continue which with time can only accelerate'.

All these different problems brought about a breakdown in the health of Mr Swinfen. After one period of absence, during which Mrs Mary Miles was Acting

Headteacher Mrs Mary Miles who took over in 1992 and has brought the building and the school back from the brink.

Head, he was seconded to serve as President of the Birmingham Association of the NUT for 1990-91. Mrs Miles was again in charge. Mr Swinfen returned in January 1991 but became ill again and took early retirement. Mrs Miles was confirmed as Head in December of that year. It proved to be the turning point in the school's fortunes. She brought vigour and energy to the job of restoring the fabric and the reputation of Moseley and, more crucially, a clear idea of how it was to be done. Following a ruthless assessment of the school's strengths and weaknesses, she laid down a clear direction for the school and set about achieving a much higher profile by attracting money and positive publicity.

The major battle was still to save the old building. No progress had been made in the years since the council's U-turn on demolition; the scaffolding remained up, at an annual cost of £5,000, while the damp and rot continued to eat away at the neglected building. The years of inaction were taking their toll on the campaigners. As those at the school became increasingly depressed, their cause was boosted by a visit in 1993 by Professor Tim Brighouse, prior to taking up his post as Chief Education Officer in Birmingham. He looked at the building, listened to the saga, and promised his support. His arrival in the city, which was to do so much for the morale of its teachers, was accompanied by a commitment from the council to restore educational spending levels. At last, perhaps, it seemed that Moseley was not going to be treated as a problem that would go away if they ignored it.

The campaign received further impetus with the 70th Anniversary reunion in 1993. This hugely successful event, organised on behalf of the school by Mrs

A chance meeting in September 1992 between Old Moseleian Mr Len Perry (centre) and teacher Mrs Gaye Key (4th from left) led to the 1993 Reunion which gave further impetus to the campaign to save West Wing.

Lost in memories .... one old Moseleian at the 1993 Reunion.

Gaye Key, showed clearly that 'students and staff, past and present, share a great pride in the school and its history'. It led to the revival in 1994 of the Act of Remembrance on Armistice Day, which now takes place every year. In April 1995, the 'new' Moseleians Association formally came into being. Its support had dwindled with the decline of its rugby teams and the loss of the Lugtrout Lane facilities. Now with initial funding from individual loans and 'a generous advance from the school', it enjoys a growing membership, a varied social programme and its own twice yearly newsletter. The Moseleians became increasingly involved in the survival of the building and the life of the present school.

The reunion 'created movement' in the campaign as so many proud Old Boys picked their way around the scaffolded remains of their former school. Then the first of several invaluable allies appeared on the scene: the city council's Buildings Engineering Supervisor, Mr Mike Miller, whose role is described as 'crucial' by Pete Anstey. This impetus led to the commissioning in 1993 of a Feasibility Study regarding the Renovation of the West Wing of Moseley School. The commission was awarded to Beard Dove Limited of Coventry, who were encouraged to tender for the work by Old Moseleian Roy Holloway, a senior employee in the firm. Their brief was to identify primary structural defects and indicate the overall extent of the deterioration, and to recommend suitable remedial measures. The survey drew on specialist advice on timber preservation and the restoration of stonework.

The Feasibility Study documented the scale of the deterioration of the building, attributing it to the longstanding problem of water ingress. This was caused by the failure of 'the detailing that ensured that the building effectively carried rainwater away' and had been exacerbated by poor maintenance. Other major problems included the 'spread' of the library roof, which was believed to have caused the external wall to move, perhaps as long ago as 100 years before. Partial remedial work had not fully resolved the problem of this 'inherent design deficiency'.

The Library, heavily scaffolded to shore wall curvature which put it out of alignment by as much as six inches, was found to have suffered heavily from water ingress, dry rot and beetle infestation. The True Dry Rot fungus was found in the nine principal roof trusses 'causing severe to complete breakdown'. The report recommended replacement of decayed roof tiles, lead flashings and aprons around chimneys, concrete fillets and stone minarets, flooring and floor joists, but concluded that the existing structural integrity could be preserved with additional supports.

The tower block could not be fully inspected because of the risk to health posed by pigeon droppings: 'if not adequately protected our men could contract diseases such as Salmonella, Ornithosis and biting insects such as fleas and bird mites' wrote the specialist preservation company. Inspection of the roof area indicated 'extensive ponding and vegetation where the timber structure has partially failed', the render of the parapet brickwork 'is both porous and broken away in large areas' and the staircase 'is engulfed in pigeon droppings' which are 'leaking through the open joints in the boarding to the soffit'. However, 'the brick structure generally appears sound', 'the stonework generally is in fair condition' and there was 'no evidence of significant movement to the tower'.

The Headmaster's House had suffered damage to timber and masonry as a result of 'considerable water penetration', 'significant woodworm infestation', pigeons and vermin. The rainwater gutters were host to 'significant vegetation .. allowing a small tree to flourish in the brickwork at one point!' The West Wing classrooms adjoining the House showed major deterioration with extensive wet rot and dry rot damage to the roof structure. As a result 'it must be considered highly desirable to carry out timber repair and replacement to this area in order that the structure can be made watertight and consequential damage to adjacent parts of the building prevented'.

The Feasibility Study identified three potential levels of repair work: minimal 'first aid' work to prevent further deterioration; work needed to allow occupation of the buildings; and restoration. The cost was estimated at £357,500 for first aid, £153,300 for the second alternative and £172,700 to complete full renovation. The study concluded that although 'in isolation the cost of the renovation works may be considered high' it was feasible to renovate the building to a suitable standard. Moreover, the cost 'must be viewed in the context of the building's historical significance, statutory obligations to preserve listed buildings and the promotional effect of retaining such a landmark'.

The relatively low cost of restoration came as a 'political bombshell' which 'embarrassed the council' because its previous repair estimates had been 'massive'. This added to the feeling of many involved in the campaign that the council had been working to a hidden agenda in relation to the school: 'there was always the feeling that someone somewhere in the council wanted the building to collapse' commented one person who had been closely involved. The report's assessment of the basic soundness of the building's structure, the clear feasibility of restoring it, and the historical and heritage significance of doing so, gave considerable encouragement to those fighting to save it.

Further impetus came from the DfEE's Surplus Place Removal Programme, and another key ally, Capital Programmes Officer Mr Peter Farrell. He spotted the potential of the DfEE programme and, with Deputy Head Pete Anstey, applied for funds. A first allocation of £300,000 was used for the refurbishment of science and technology facilities, a second of the same amount formed part of the budget for repair work on the gym and assembly hall. Peter Farrell was also instrumental in identifying European programmes as a potential source of funds.

Building work under way at last. The roof of the gymnasium (shown here) and of the assembly hall were the first to be done.

Had these events occurred five years earlier, or even five years later, it is very possible that Moseley School's Victorian heritage would now be a pile of rubble, as Councillor Eames had so graciously described it, or indeed vanished without trace under a new development. However, the early nineties coincided with the introduction of substantial European funding programmes and, even better, 'the concept of the lottery was on the horizon'. With help from Peter Farrell and a new ally, Mr David Ritchie of the Regional Government Office, funding bids were prepared to finance the saving of the building. David Ritchie worked through the council's European Office Committee to submit a city council application to the European Regional Development Fund, of which £966,000 to repair the Moseley building was a part.

Mr Chris Ryle and Mr Will Howland of the City Architect's Department also came on board the campaign and proved to be key players in its success. They became convinced of the importance of the building's 'major architectural value' and targeted the new National Lottery Heritage Fund as its possible saviour. An application was submitted in January 1995 in the first ever round of grant awards. Pete Anstey recalls how 'nothing happened' for seven months, generating 'huge anxiety' and 'panic' amongst the applicants. But the Heritage Fund was finding its feet and had at that time no mechanism in place for processing bids. Eventually, representatives of the fund visited Moseley and 'became enthusiastic on seeing the building'. A return visit by Pete Anstey and the architects confirmed an optimistic prospect for the bid.

In fact, the Heritage Fund administrators became so enthusiastic that they proposed awarding more money than the school had asked for, in order to land-scape the grounds around the building. During the process of assessing the application, they sought an expert appraisal of the heritage value from architectural historian David Walker. His report, produced in September 1996, sketched the history of the building and analysed it architecturally. His assessment was unambiguously favourable:

> *Spring Hill College is an excellent building of its date and an extra-ordinary performance for a man of twenty-five. Keble apart, it is as good as any of the early Victorian college buildings in Oxford or Cambridge, if less expensively built than some. Even giving due weight to the somewhat destructive alterations to the east and west wings in 1923, its unstarred grading at II is a nonsense.*

The report described Spring Hill as 'a design full of interesting and original ideas' and itemised several of them in the central tower – 'a very deep portal with fine carving, inscribed wafer thin sub-arch ... clever and effective lighting of the entrance hall ... the shapely transition of the oriels from the rectangular to the canted'. It further notes that 'throughout the remainder of the building the details are of equally high quality'. The building, declares David Walker, is 'probably the best surviving work' of 'one of the ablest architects of his generation' and despite a considerable number of early Victorian buildings of the same general design 'only a handful, mostly for universities or the grandest public schools, have comparable qualities'.

As well as 'warmly recommending' the College to the Trustees of the Heritage Fund, the report advocates even more restoration of original features than the funding application sought. It also states that 'A long-term conservation plan for the further restoration and enhancement of the building should be developed and should be enshrined in the grant offer.' Addressing the Fund's criteria which excluded 'the development, repair or maintenance of schools', David Walker concludes that 'Spring Hill College is much too important a building to be lost on too narrow an interpretation of the guidelines.'

On 12 December 1996, a jubilant Mary Miles told the Birmingham Post:

> *We are finally able to celebrate 18 months of hard work having secured sufficient money to restore one of Birmingham's finest landmark buildings.*

The Heritage Fund had awarded £2.25 million which, added to the £995,000 of Education money, £966,000 from the European Regional Development Fund and £405,000 from Birmingham City Council, provided the £4.6 million restoration budget. The Heritage grant formed the bulk of the West Midlands' £3.8 million Heritage Lottery award and was a great vindication of the determination of those who had fought to save the building.

While the restoration work went on apace, Mary Miles was able to return her full attention to the running of Moseley School. Her vision and ambition for the school have borne fruit in the seven years since she acceded to the headship. A colleague observes:

> *Mrs Miles has, I think, done a marvellous job in a challenging situation, hammering away at Moseley to create a new school with a high profile, helped as always at Moseley by an excellent staff.*

Moseley received a resounding vote of confidence from the OFSTED Inspection Team which inspected the school in spring 1995. The quality of the experience offered to Moseley pupils was recognised in its report:

> Moseley School is a good school with clear aims which it constantly, and in the main effectively, strives to meet. It adds considerable value to the achievements of its pupils. ... The school provides a caring, orderly, good-natured and harmonious learning environment, with a wide range of links with the local community. ... The headteacher has a very well developed understanding of her role in leading the school. ... There is open and broadly effective management at all levels which motivate staff well. ... The quality of teaching is at least sound and often good or very good. ... The quality of learning was sound or better in 81 per cent of the lessons observed.

Despite the predominance of boys, the report found that 'girls feel safe and valued', and that 'the behaviour of the pupils is good. The school is a good-humoured and orderly community'. There are a few very minor criticisms contained in the report but it overwhelmingly endorses the school's standards and priorities.

The school pioneered vocational education ....

.... and information technology

Moseley School now has a clear sense of purpose, a modernised curriculum and a full programme of cultural and educational activities. Recognition of the social and linguistic disadvantage that many of its pupils bring to school has led to a conscious attempt to provide them with a compensatory level of confidence and expertise in areas like information technology and vocational training. A Sixth Form team recently came second in the finals of the National Investment Programme held at the Stock Exchange and involving 1,100 teams. In 1992 Moseley won the Schools Curriculum Award for Equal Entitlement and the school's public profile was further raised by the award of the Government's Charter Mark in 1996, the first to a Birmingham school.

There is a continuous programme of visits in Britain and abroad to widen pupils' experience. The school cottage is in use for most of the year. There are concerts and arts and drama projects every year, as well as a variety of sporting opportunities. Cricket in particular benefits from the school's link with the Attock Cricket Club which has dramatically improved the facilities available, using funding from the Sports Council. The opening of the complex in 1995 featured a match against a celebrity X1 which included Mustaq Mohammed and Alvin Kallicharan. Unlike most state schools, cricket at Moseley is flourishing. There have also been some outstanding achievements by the girls' netball teams.

Moseley School's successful cricketers receive their prize – new equipment – from Warwickshire and England cricketer Gladstone Small, himself a former pupil of the school.

Work on the exciting new Health and Fitness centre will soon be finished, along with an all-weather floodlit hockey pitch, the fruits of another successful bid to the Sports Council Lottery Fund worth £1,679,000. Both facilities will serve the school and the local community. Another grant of £53,450 from the Government Cycle Challenge and Birmingham City Council has been used to develop safe cycle routes around the school, secure cycle storage and rider training.

Another sign of changing times. The school caretaker has been replaced by the senior Building Services Supervisor. When the school gained control of its budget, Gloria Lightwood began studying for an HNC in Business Studies and Management.

After so many years of frustration and stalemate, the renovation of the old Victorian building proceeded with impressive speed, though not without its problems. The rediscovery of the old well incurred additional costs and delays; improved information about original designs and the actual condition of sections of the building led to design changes as the work proceeded. The restoration work revealed that the original materials of the building had survived well and that most of the problems were caused by deterioration in the alterations made in the 1920s conversion to Moseley Secondary School.

However, none of the problems proved insurmountable and in the autumn of 1998, the building stands restored to its former splendour. Indeed it has probably not looked so handsome since the young would-be ministers bent to their studies or the fashionable Victorians promenaded in the Botanical Gardens. The face of the building has lost its twentieth century grime and the warm peachy brickwork glows new. The 'unusual and interesting ideas' in the design of the building have been restored with the help of some architectural detective work and the pinnacles, gargoyles, turrets and tracery have been reconstructed by contemporary experts.

Internally, the building regains its elegance, the lofty ceilings and soaring arches providing an inspiring environment for new generations of learners. With nice symmetry, it also reverts to its original name, Spring Hill College.

The buttress to the right of the tower now fully restored.

The College, for post-16 students and the community, provides opportunities for lifelong learning with a wide range of exam courses: A Levels, GNVQs, key skill accreditation and courses in information technology, business, health and social care, science, manufacturing, leisure and tourism. It is equipped with state of the art computers, with access to the internet and email in all rooms, and has video-conferencing facilities. It will be a centre for the community and business, offering facilities for conferences and meetings, and for large social and arts events.

The building has now emerged from its cocoon of scaffolding to reveal details hidden for years by dirt and decay.

This splendid new facility will add immeasurably to the opportunities offered by Moseley School, which can now look to the future with high expectations and a sense of accomplishment against the odds. The twin themes of innovation and fine tradition will be familiar to many who knew the school of old. In the late 1990s, the school has once again a strong headteacher, committed and loyal staff, enthusiastic and hardworking pupils, and a happy and positive atmosphere. The re-opening of Spring Hill College heralds an exciting new phase in Moseley's distinguished history, in which its proud traditions of endeavour and achievement will encompass educational and social opportunities for the whole community.

The first Spring Hill College was born out of the Nonconformist movement, whose core belief was that responsibility lies with the congregation and not with hierarchies of power. It is fitting that its second incarnation under that name was achieved only through the action of ordinary people challenging the decisions of those in authority, and that the grand Victorian building is now reborn to serve the needs and interests of the communities of Moseley, Sparkhill and beyond. It is also fitting that an institution created through innovation and invention in mid-nineteenth century England should uphold its groundbreaking tradition and look ahead to becoming a state of the art centre of excellence in the new Millennium.

References and acknowledgements

The chapter draws on the following reports: City Architect's Department 'Moseley School: Investigation of the Building's Defects and Delapidation' (1986) and 'Assessment of the Deterioration in the Condition of the West Wing since mid 1986' (1990); Beard Dove Limited 'The Feasibility Study regarding the Renovation of the West Wing of Moseley School for Birmingham City Council' (1993); David Walker 'Spring Hill College, Moseley, Birmingham: Heritage Merit' (1996); David Leeson 'Moseley School' in Birmingham 13 magazine; Spring Hill College Moseley Conservation Plan prepared for the Heritage Lottery Fund; The Birmingham Post and Evening Mail; miscellaneous council papers, correspondence and other documents. The accounts of David Hebden and Pete Anstey have been particularly valuable and help has also been given by John Lockwood, Mary Miles, Betty Gillespie, Steve Rosson, Malcolm Cook, Brian Miles, Pete Samuels, John Webb and Becky Hopkins (nee Wyatt). Thanks to Roy Holloway and Angela Billingham for the loan of photographs and Birmingham Design Services for architects' drawings.

The Story in Brief

1838 Spring Hill College opens in the former home of Mrs Sarah Glover and her sister for the training of Nonconformist ministers.

1851 The family purchases land at Moseley Wake Green for the building of a new college. The design of Joseph James is chosen.

1857 Spring Hill College opens its doors.

1870 An Act of Parliament sets up School Boards.

1886 Spring Hill College moves to Oxford and becomes known as Mansfield College.

1892 Mr William Ross buys the Spring Hill site and buildings, and develops it as the Pine Dell Hydropathic Establishment and Moseley Botanical Gardens.

1900 Pine Dell closes. The Ross family continues to live there.

1900 Yardley School Board opens College Road Board School.

1902 School Boards are abolished. Worcestershire County Council takes over the management of College Road.

1911 Yardley is incorporated into the Borough of Birmingham. Control of College Road School passes to Birmingham.

1914 Spring Hill is requisitioned as a military barracks for training the 3rd Birmingham City Battalion of the Royal Warwickshire Regiment.

1921 The buildings are used for a special teacher training course for partially disabled ex-servicemen, under the name Springfield College.

1923 Birmingham Education Authority acquires Spring Hill for conversion to a secondary school. Mr E. H. Robinson is appointed Headmaster of the new Moseley Secondary School.

1924 The East Wing is adapted as a gymnasium.

1927 New specialist rooms are built at College Road to provide facilities for older pupils.

1927 A new Science wing is built at Moseley adjoining the East Wing.

1928 The Obelisk is transported to Mansfield College.

1934   College Road School is reorganised as Infants, Junior Mixed and Senior Mixed departments.

1939   Moseley Secondary School is renamed Moseley Grammar School.

1939   Over half of Moseley's pupils are evacuated to Cheltenham. College Road pupils are also evacuated. Both groups return after a few months.

1940   Moseley is damaged by bombs and the boys evacuated to Kidderminster. College Road also suffers bomb damage and the children are evacuated to Loughborough.

1942   Both schools reopen but with fewer pupils.

1944   The Butler Education Act paves the way for the introduction of Grammar, Technical and Secondary Modern Schools.

1950   The war memorial is unveiled at Moseley Grammar School.

1953   The first group of children sits the 11-plus examination.

1954   A new block containing Art and Technical rooms and a dining hall is added at Moseley Grammar School.

1955   Moseley Modern Mixed School opens under Headteacher Miss E. Cohen.

1956   Mr D. B. Gaskin is appointed to the Headship of Moseley Grammar School following Mr Robinson's retirement.

1965   A government circular invites Local Education Authorities to submit plans for comprehensive reorganisation.

1965   Moseley Grammar School finishes building its pavilion.

1967   Mr D. Wilford is appointed to succeed Miss Cohen (now Mrs North).

1968   The controlling Labour Group on Birmingham City Council publishes plans for comprehensive schooling.

1968   Moseley Grammar School acquires the 'school cottage' in Wales.

1970   The Conservatives take control of the council and produce counter proposals for the city's schools.

1972   The council swings to Labour again. A motion to abolish selection is quickly passed.

1972   Moseley Grammar School is listed as a building of Special Architectural and Historical Interest.

1973   Mr D. G. Moore is appointed Acting Head of Moseley Grammar School on the retirement of Mr Gaskin.

1973 Birmingham's plans for reorganisation are rejected by the Secretary of State for Education.

1974 Moseley Modern School takes possession of its much-needed extension.

1974 The amalgamation of Moseley Grammar School and Moseley Modern School finally goes ahead. Mr A. Goodfellow is appointed as Head of the new Moseley School.

1982 Mr Goodfellow dies following a series of heart attacks. Mr D. M. Swinfen is appointed to succeed him.

1984 Problems are discovered in the condition of the original Victorian building, the school's West Wing.

1986 A major part of West Wing including the Library is closed on grounds of safety.

1987 Birmingham Education Committee announces proposals to demolish the building. These are quickly withdrawn in the face of public opposition. The school begins trying to raise funds for repair work.

1988 Education Act introduces major changes in the running of schools.

1992 Mrs M. Miles is appointed to succeed Mr Swinfen whose health has broken down.

1992 Moseley School wins the Schools Curriculum Award.

1993 Professor Tim Brighouse is appointed Chief Education Officer for Birmingham.

1996 Moseley School becomes the first in Birmingham to receive the Government's Charter Mark.

1996 The school wins Lottery funding for a new Health and Fitness Centre to be shared with the community.

1996 The Heritage Lottery Fund and the European Regional Development Fund jointly agree to fund the complete restoration of West Wing and the development of Spring Hill Sixth Form College. Work starts immediately.

1998 The Victorian building, gloriously restored and in newly landscaped grounds, finally comes back into use, for post-16 education and community use.

Postscript

As Moseley School celebrates the survival of its historic building and looks ahead to a dynamic future, the aspirations of the present generation of students are voiced by Sixth-former Shaziah Khan, who won the 1998 Cambridge University Young Black Achievers award with this poem:

OUR GRADUATION DAY

My only burning desire in life is
to be successful and go to university.

What motivates me, keeps me full of hope
is a picture which I've painted at the back of my mind
and under my eyelids.

It's a picture of me on my *graduation day*.

The beautiful sky-blue background and the black gown and hat
which I've presumably hired for the day.

I know I always look good in black
but my true beauty shall sparkle through my smile
the day I wear these garments for the first and last time in my life.

My eyes shall drown in dewdrops and the sound of their delicate drip
will announce my happiness to the world.

My lips shall create the happiest smile lips have ever smiled
and without a sound they'll express the joy of my soul.

What I have lived for, and that which I live for is this one and only tomorrow
and when this tomorrow arrives there will be no other day like it.

My graduation will symbolise the death of this present ambition
and engender the birth of a new desire.

This ambition, achieved by success, will lead to a new dream.
What this dream shall be, yet I don't know and how will I transform it to reality
is also a beautiful mystery.

But, what I do know is that I have a promise to fulfil
and a duty to perform.

Step by step shall I climb the ladder of success
so I *must* be confident and believe in myself.

I'm aware life has a tariff on every ambition
but I'll pay it off with my invincible motivation.

When I set eyes on the many unlettered
Brown faces of mothers and sisters;
who are victims, deprived of independence and literacy.,

Then my coloured soul grieves to see such worthy ones being pitied.
Many are not heard for they speak in a foreign voice and others are subtly
not seen equal for they do not have colourless skin.

But when I look up, aching my neck
I see heaven, so called achievement.
Then this being within me yells *come on!*
you can do it.
You can dwell in that paradise one day
and many Brown faces will follow in the same way.

All I have to remember is the gown, the hat, the colourful smiles
on my, yours, no! *OUR graduation day.*

By Shaziah Khan